FACTS AT YOUR FINGERTIPS

WORLD WAR I

FACTS AT YOUR FINGERTIPS

WORLD WAR I

WAYLAND

This edition published in 2013 by Wayland

Copyright © Brown Bear Books Limited 2013

Wayland
Hachette Children's Books
338 Euston Road
London NW1 3BH

Wayland Australia
Level 17/207 Kent Street
Sydney NSW 2000

Brown Bear Books Limited
Editorial Director: Lindsey Lowe
Managing Editor: Tim Cooke
Creative Director: Jeni Child
Picture Manager: Sophie Mortimer
Production: Richard Berry
Indexer: Indexing Specialists (UK) Ltd

British Library Cataloguing in Publication Data
Westwell, Ian.
   World War I. – (Facts at your fingertips)
   1. World War, 1914-1918–Juvenile literature.
   I. Title II. Series
   940.4-dc22

ISBN 978 0 7502 7941 3

10 9 8 7 6 5 4 3 2 1

Printed in the United States of America

Wayland is a division of Hachette Children's Books,
an Hachette UK company.
www.hachette.co.uk

Websites
The website addresses (URLs) included in this book were valid at the time of going to press. However, because of the nature of the Internet, it is possible that some addresses may have changed, or sites may have changed or closed down since publication. While the author and publisher regret any inconvenience this may cause readers, no responsibility for any such changes can be accepted by either the author or the publisher.

Picture acknowledgements
All images Robert Hunt Library

Cover Images
Front: U.S. troops during the Meuse–Argonne Offensive in 1918 (Robert Hunt Library)
Back: Australian infantrymen await the order to attack the Turks at Gallipoli (Robert Hunt Library)
Page 3: Australian troops advance at Gallipoli (Robert Hunt Library)

CONTENTS

Introduction   **6**

1914   **8**

1915   **22**

1916   **34**

1917   **44**

1918   **54**

Further Resources   **63**

Index   **64**

World War I's origins dated back to the last quarter of the 19th century. The world's leading powers, particularly in Europe, began a dangerous game of political brinkmanship. The major rivals were Austria-Hungary, Britain, France, Germany and Russia. They all tried to extend their international influence, motivated by rampant nationalism, economic expansion, a scramble to acquire colonies and the pursuit of military prestige.

Colonialism, the domination of an area and its people by another state, was often driven by a belief than one race was superior to another. European colonists thought that they were somehow superior, and that they had the right to take the territory of peoples they considered inferior. Colonies also played an important economic role as sources of raw material or as markets for goods manufactured at home.

Valuable colonies

Colonial expansion got into its stride in the second half of the 19th century. In 1870 European powers controlled some 70 percent of the globe; by 1914 the figure was 85 percent. Europe's interest was centred on Africa, which had previously escaped major colonisation.

By the latter part of the 19th century it was clear that new colonies were becoming increasingly difficult to find. The leading powers were coming into conflict – if not outright war – with each other as each attempted to grab areas ripe for colonisation. In 1898 Britain and France came close to conflict when a French expedition marched into Fashoda, a town in British-controlled Sudan. In 1911 Germany sent a gunboat to Agadir in Morocco, which had recently been taken over by the French, to challenge France's right to the country.

The arms race

The scramble for colonies was parallelled by a European arms race. The powers needed to protect their far-flung territories, secure their trade with them and maintain a balance of military power with their neighbours in Europe. None of the powers was willing to see another gain an unassailable military advantage. The arms race coincided with rapid industrialisation and innovation in military technologies. Weapons were becoming increasingly powerful, more deadly and available in huge numbers thanks to standardisation and mass production.

Colonial, economic and military rivalries impacted on the balance of power that regulated the relationships between Europe's leading nations. In the past, if one nation gained an advantage of some type, its chief rival or rivals would act to negate the advantage in one way or another. The European balance of power depended on no single nation or nations being able to gain an unassailable lead.

German troops on manoeuvres in the years before the outbreak of World War I. The German Army was an excellent fighting force that had modern weapons and high morale.

By the beginning of the 20th century it was clear that Britain and Germany had moved far ahead of their rivals. Germany was militarily superior on land, had a dynamic industrial base and was intent on extending its power in Europe. Meanwhile Britain was the largest colonial power, had the most powerful navy and a strong, if declining, industrial base.

Allies and rivals

Before the outbreak of World War I, Europe's powers had entered into a series of often-shifting alliances with each other.

Germany became allied with Austria-Hungary, the two known as the Central Powers. Allied against them were Britain, France and Russia – the Triple Entente. These networks of alliances, both informal and formal, effectively guaranteed that an attack on one alliance member was considered an attack on them all.

All the European powers were aware of the network of alliances, and most developed war plans based on the understanding that, once a war broke out between any two rival alliance members, the others would react immediately. Thus it became necessary to develop plans for the rapid mobilisation of armies and their swift movement, usually by rail, to the front line.

The flashpoint between the two alliances was the Balkans, a region split by ethnic divisions and nationalistic aspirations. Turkey's influence in the region was declining, and both Austria-Hungary and Russia – members of rival alliances – had imperial ambitions there. Serbia, whose security was guaranteed by Russia, was a particularly ambitious local power. It was determined to establish a 'Greater Serbia'.

The security of Austria-Hungary, the weaker of the Central Powers, was guaranteed by Germany. Indeed, Kaiser Wilhelm II had told his planners to prepare for

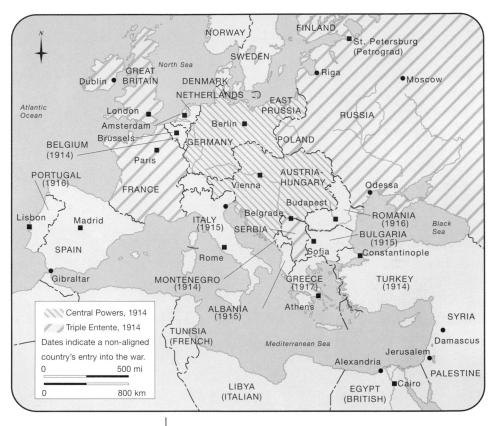

war in late 1912 to early 1913, when a local conflict in the Balkans saw Serbia gain territory from Turkey and threaten Austro-Hungarian possessions in the northern Adriatic. Austria-Hungary, backed by Germany, declared that it would go to war if Serbia did not give up its gains. Such a move would have prompted a Russian response, thereby drawing in France. Serbia did back down. However, a possible route for a local conflict to spark a Europe-wide war had been revealed. On both sides, some people who were confident of victory actively wanted war to come.

It was not long before a similar incident did trigger war. On 28 June, 1914, the heir to the Austro-Hungarian throne, Archduke Ferdinand, was assassinated by a Serb nationalist while visiting Sarajevo, the capital of Bosnia, an Austro-Hungarian province.

In 1914 most countries, their civilians and politicians alike, believed that they were going to war for the right reasons. War enthusiasm was everywhere – but it would die, along with many thousands of troops, in the trenches during the first year of war.

To many people in Europe the outbreak of war in August 1914 was a welcome opportunity to put right perceived wrongs in international relations. Governments were just as eager as their citizens. All the great powers had plans they believed would ensure that the war would end in their favour – and quickly.

In 1893 France and Russia signed a military alliance that greatly alarmed Germany's chief of the General Staff, Count Alfred von Schlieffen. Schlieffen was acutely aware of the dangers of Germany fighting a major war on two fronts. He saw France as the most immediate threat in any conflict involving the three countries. He therefore developed a plan to knock France out of any war in a matter of weeks before Russia could mobilise its vast armies.

The Schlieffen Plan

Schlieffen realised that France's border defences with Germany were far too strong to be taken quickly, and that rapid movement through Switzerland's mountainous terrain was impossible. His plan therefore depended on sending a massive force, some 90 percent of the total German Army, through Belgium and Holland, to then swing south towards Paris. Both Belgium and Holland were neutral countries, however, whose neutrality was guaranteed by other powers.

Meanwhile, five percent of the German Army would defend Alsace-Lorraine, where Schlieffen expected – and wanted – the French forces to attack. The region's strong border fortifications, backed by a resolute defence, would tie up a large part of the French Army.

The loss of Alsace-Lorraine had been France's greatest humiliation following its defeat at the hands of Germany in the Franco-Prussian War (1870–1871). France had long expected to go to war with Germany again in the future and its military leaders developed a war strategy to win back the lost provinces.

Between 1911 and 1914, General Joseph Joffre, the French commander-in-chief, devised Plan XVII. It called for the various French armies to assemble along the key frontier from Switzerland to Belgium and launch an

A German 17in howitzer is readied for action. It could lob a large shell accurately to a range of 9,140 metres (10,000 yards).

immediate, devastating attack in strength into Alsace-Lorraine. Joffre recognised that the Germans might violate Belgium's neutrality in an attack on France, but believed that they could not advance past the Meuse River in northeast France without becoming dangerously overextended. The French also had an informal arrangement with Britain that guaranteed that a British army would be available to plug any gap on the Franco-Belgian border.

Plan XVII had two key weaknesses. First, Joffre underestimated the quality of the German Army and the speed with which it could mobilise and move. Second, the French adhered to the doctrine of constant attack. They believed that a resolute attack could fight through any defence. Instead, as they learned in 1914, resolute attacks in the face of defensive machine-gun fire could lead to very heavy casualties for little gain.

Russia and Austro-Hungary

The war plans of both the Austro-Hungarians and Russians were designed to fit with Germany's war strategy. Austria-Hungary had two plans. First, there was the strategy known as Plan B to fight in the Balkans, with Serbia as the enemy. Second, Plan R had been developed to fight on two fronts against both Serbia and its ally, Russia.

Russia also had two war plans. First, if Germany attacked Russia, the Russian armies would fight a defensive war. If, however, Germany chose to attack France first, Russian troops would march into East Prussia as quickly as possible.

Uniquely, Britain was the only major European power that did not have some form of conscription at the outbreak of World War I. Its regular army, although much smaller than its European counterparts, was an all-volunteer force. Man for man, it was probably the best. Its regular infantry regiments were highly trained, skilled in most aspects of warfare and renowned for the volume and accuracy of their rifle fire.

At the outset of the war Britain's greatest contribution was its powerful navy of more than 500 vessels. In the key area of dreadnought battleships and battlecruisers, the British naval forces enjoyed a 28:18 superiority over Germany's High Seas Fleet.

Southeast of Metz, two French armies, the First under General Auguste Dubail and the Second commanded by General Noël de Castelnau, attacked into Lorraine, initiating the first of a series of engagements that become known as the 'Battle of the Frontiers'.

Two German armies made a slow but coordinated withdrawal to give time for reinforcements to arrive. The German counterattack on 20 August forced the French back. The Battle of the Frontiers then switched to the wooded Ardennes region north of Metz. Two French armies advancing at speed into Belgium ran into two German armies rushing through Luxembourg and southeast Belgium on the 22nd. Three days of confused fighting followed, with the outnumbered French blunting the German attacks and launching their own counterattacks. French losses were severe. The French, pursued by the Germans, fell back to positions between the Meuse and Marne rivers.

In the third engagement of the Battle of the Frontiers the French commander-in-chief, General Joseph Joffre, ordered General Charles Lanrezac's Fifth Army to halt the German advance. The French suffered very high casualties. Lanrezac sought and was granted permission by Joffre to withdraw.

The British Expeditionary Force took part in the final encounter of the Battle of the Frontiers, at Mons (see page 12).

In August 1914 two Russian forces, the First Army under General Pavel Rennenkampf and General Alexander Samsonov's Second Army, invaded East Prussia from the east and southeast, where they were met by General Max von Prittwitz's thinly spread Eighth Army. However, the Russian armies were widely separated, chiefly by the Masurian Lakes, and were lacking in most types of equipment. Prittwitz's troops, although overstretched and outnumbered, acted as a delaying force.

On 17 August, German forces inflicted a defeat on Rennenkampf's advance guard at Stallupönen, causing 3,000 casualties and pushing the Russians back to the East Prussian frontier. The German commander at Stallupönen, General Hermann von Francois, then fell back to Gumbinnen.

Russian troops in a Polish town prepare to march to the front. Many Russian troops lacked ammunition and equipment.

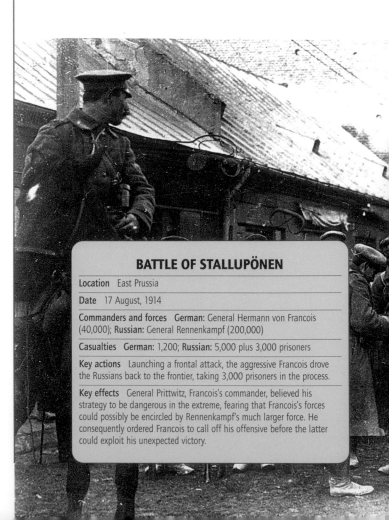

BATTLE OF THE FRONTIERS

Location Lorraine, the Ardennes and southern Belgium

Date 14-24 August, 1914

Commanders and forces **German:** Helmuth von Moltke (1,300,000); **British:** Sir John French (70,000); **French:** Joseph Joffre (1,200,000)

Casualties **German:** 300,000; **French:** 300,000; **British:** 1,600

Key actions On 23 August the Battle of Mons began when Kluck's divisions blundered into the British II Corps of 36,000 men behind the Mons Canal between Mons and Conde on the French border. Accurate British rifle fire stopped the German advance, but the French were retreating on the British right, and Sir John French ordered a British retreat on 24 August.

Key effects The Schlieffen Plan, while still on course, was beginning to come to pieces under the tentative control of Moltke. The opening of the Russian offensive in East Prussia and the unforeseen attack in Lorraine had drained the German right wing that was descending on Paris. Von Kluck's decision to take his First Army east of the French capital exposed his right flank, which the Allies exploited in the First Battle of the Marne in early September, halting the German advance.

BATTLE OF STALLUPÖNEN

Location East Prussia

Date 17 August, 1914

Commanders and forces **German:** General Hermann von Francois (40,000); **Russian:** General Rennenkampf (200,000)

Casualties **German:** 1,200; **Russian:** 5,000 plus 3,000 prisoners

Key actions Launching a frontal attack, the aggressive Francois drove the Russians back to the frontier, taking 3,000 prisoners in the process.

Key effects General Prittwitz, Francois's commander, believed his strategy to be dangerous in the extreme, fearing that Francois's forces could possibly be encircled by Rennenkampf's much larger force. He consequently ordered Francois to call off his offensive before the latter could exploit his unexpected victory.

BATTLE OF GUMBINNEN

At Gumbinnen, the Germans, who feared encirclement, confronted the slowly advancing Russian forces of General Rennenkampf. General Hermann von Francois, who acted decisively, unlike the dithering Prittwitz, drove Rennenkampf back some 8 kilometres (5 miles). However, other German attacks were unsuccessful. Prittwitz was relieved of his command and was replaced by the elderly General Paul von Hindenburg, who was recalled from retirement. Hindenburg's chief-of-staff was confirmed as the dynamic General Erich Ludendorff, fresh from his role in capturing the crucial Belgian frontier fortress of Liège.

BATTLE OF GUMBINNEN

Location   East Prussia

Date   20 August, 1914

Commanders and forces   German: General von Prittwitz (150,000); Russian: General Rennenkampf (200,000)

Casualties   German: 14,800; Russian: 16,500

Key actions   Effective Russian siting of heavy artillery wreaked havoc among the German XVII Corps, forcing it to withdraw some 24 km (15 miles) in disorder. Francois, aware that the German centre and right were in disarray, was forced to order a retreat.

Key effects   Pritwitz ordered a general withdrawal to the Vistula River, effectively conceding East Prussia to the Russians.

SIEGE OF NAMUR

Belgian civilians look on as a German supply column prepares to move out toward Namur in August 1914.

The city of Namur was ringed by a number of forts. It was believed that the forts, nine in total, plus infantry, would protect the Sambre and Meuse rivers against German invasion.

With the fall of Liège on 16 August, 1914, the German Second and Third Armies, led by General von Bulow, turned their attention to Namur. The garrison at Namur intended to hold out until the arrival of the French Fifth Army, which deployed across the River Sambre to the southwest.

Following a day of probing attacks upon Fort de Marchovelette on 20 August, the German Second Army began firing upon the forts in earnest the next day. In part to divert the French Fifth Army away from the forts, the bulk of the German Second Army launched an attack on the French at Charleroi. The strategy was successful. Only one unit of infantry from the Fifth Army, the 45th Brigade, was sent to assist with the defence of Namur.

The Belgian garrison, with little hope of being relieved and being pounded by heavy siege guns, surrendered on 23 August.

SIEGE OF NAMUR

Location   Belgium

Date   20-23 August, 1914

Commanders and forces   German: Second and Third Armies (General von Bulow—107,000); Belgian: 37,000

Casualties   unknown

Key actions   The Germans bombarded the forts with heavy artillery, including the powerful Big Bertha gun (a 420mm siege howitzer).

Key effects   Upon hearing news of the fall of Namur, the French General Lanrezac ordered a withdrawal of his troops from the Sambre at Charleroi.

BATTLE OF MONS

A British cavalry unit falls back after briefly slowing the pace of the German attack at the Battle of Mons.

At Mons, in the final encounter of the Battle of the Frontiers, the British Expeditionary Force (BEF) fought General Alexander von Kluck's German First Army. Although heavily outnumbered the British repulsed the first German attack, inflicting severe casualties with accurate and high-volume rifle fire. Subsequent German attacks forced the British back just 5 kilometres (3 miles). Because of the withdrawal of Lanrezac's French Fifth Army a little to the east, the British were forced to conduct an orderly retreat.

Mons marked the end of the Battle of the Frontiers. To Helmuth von Moltke, the German chief-of-staff, this sprawling series of battles seemed to herald a great victory. French casualties were high (some 300,000 men), and both they and the British were in a seemingly disorganised retreat.

BATTLE OF MONS

Location Belgium

Date 23 August, 1914

Commanders and forces   German: First Army (General Alexander von Kluck – 160,000); **British:** British Expeditionary Force (General Sir John French – 70,000)

Casualties   German: 5,000; **British:** 1,600

Key actions Von Kluck's attack following a preliminary artillery barrage began disastrously, the British riflemen exacting heavy losses from the advancing German infantry.

Key effects The British wanted to resume the battle on 24 August, but to the east the French were still retreating. A dangerous gap was beginning to open up between the BEF and the French Fifth Army, and so on the morning of the 24th French was forced to order a general retreat. This retreat would last for two weeks, and would cost the BEF many more casualties than had fallen at Mons.

BATTLE OF LE CATEAU

As the British Expeditionary Force continued to retreat south across northeast France, it fought almost constant rearguard actions against General Alexander von Kluck's First Army. At Le Cateau the British II Corps, under General Smith-Dorrien, fought for survival as the Germans attempted to surround it.

During the morning of 26 August, the British, notably the field artillery, held overwhelming numbers of the enemy at bay and inflicted severe losses. The corps then disengaged and withdrew south during the afternoon. Smith-Dorrien's decision to stand against the Germans at Le Cateau paid off handsomely. Serious losses were inflicted on the Germans and another delay imposed on their Paris timetable. To the east, I Corps was able to move further away from the Germans. However, a rift grew between Sir John French (who had initially ordered Smith-Dorrien to continue to retreat) and Smith-Dorrien as a result of the action.

BATTLE OF LE CATEAU

Location France

Date 26–27 August, 1914

Commanders and forces   German: First Army (General von Kluck); **British:** British Expeditionary Force (General Sir John French – 40,000)

Casualties   German: 7,500; **British:** 7,800

Key actions Fighting predominantly with rifles firing from shallow trenches prepared hastily, the British managed to greatly slow the advance of the German infantry.

Key effects The heavy losses at Le Cateau and at Mons seriously demoralised Field Marshal Sir John French. For most of the period between Le Cateau and the First Battle of the Marne he was convinced that the BEF would need to be withdrawn from the line to recover.

A French 75mm field gun in action against the Germans on the Western Front in August 1914.

BATTLE OF TANNENBERG

On 24 August, German troops successfully delayed General Samsonov's advance in southern East Prussia in a day-long battle at Orlau-Frankenau. This allowed other German units to concentrate at nearby Tannenberg for their forthcoming battle against Samsonov. The Russian high command remained unaware that its uncoded radio traffic was being intercepted by the Germans.

Two days later, the Germans struck at Samsonov's Second Army outside Tannenberg from the north and south, and also in the centre. By nightfall on the 29th Samsonov had been surrounded and he is believed to have committed suicide. Attempts by Rennenkampf in the north to come to the aid of Samsonov's beleaguered forces failed. Tannenberg was a major German victory. Russian losses were enormous: the invasion of East Prussia was decisively defeated.

BATTLE OF TANNENBERG

Location East Prussia

Date 26–31 August, 1914

Commanders and forces **German:** Eighth Army (General Paul von Hindenburg – 150,000); **Russian:** Second Army (General Alexander Samsonov – 190,000), First Army (General Pavel von Rennenkampf – 210,000)

Casualties **German:** 20,000: **Russian:** 30,000 plus 95,000 wounded

Key actions On 28 August, Samsonov finally became aware that his army was surrounded. Critically short of supplies and with his communications system in tatters, his forces were dispersed. Consequently he ordered a general withdrawal on the evening of 28 August. But it was too late. Samsonov, lost in the surrounding forests with his aides, shot himself, unable to face reporting the scale of the disaster to the tsar, Nicholas II.

Key effects The scale of the Russian defeat shocked Russia's allies, who wondered whether it signalled the defeat of the Russian Army. No Russian army would penetrate into German territory again in the war.

BATTLE OF HELIGOLAND BIGHT

In August 1914, British cruisers launched a foray into German waters as part of a plan to lure elements of the German High Seas Fleet into an unequal fight, and also to prevent German warships from attacking convoys transporting follow-on units of the British Expeditionary Force across the English Channel to France. The engagement, known as the Battle of Heligoland Bight, began at 07:00 hours on 28 August. British light cruisers and destroyers under Commodore Tyrwhitt caught the Germans by surprise.

The Germans strike back

As the Germans recovered from their surprise, their more powerful warships got up steam and sailed out from their anchorage in the Jade River to attack the British. The German warships threatened to inflict severe losses, but the sudden arrival of reinforcements, chiefly five battle cruisers under Admiral Sir David Beatty, covered the withdrawal of the initial British force. No British ships were sunk during the battle, while four German vessels were sent to the bottom.

The battle was seen as a clear-cut success by the British. However, their euphoria masked severe shortcomings, particularly in the planning and conduct of complex multiforce naval operations. However, the British raid had a profound impact on the morale of the German high command. Kaiser Wilhelm II warned his naval commanders that the High Seas Fleet, already outnumbered by the British Navy, could not afford such losses. Plans to use the High Seas Fleet in large-scale offensive operations in the North Sea were shelved.

BATTLE OF HELIGOLAND BIGHT

Location North Sea

Date 28 August, 1914

Commanders and forces **German:** Rear Admiral Franz Hipper (6 light cruisers, 19 torpedo boats, 12 minesweepers); **British:** Admiral Sir David Beatty (5 battle cruisers, 8 light cruisers, 33 destroyers, 8 submarines)

Casualties **German:** 1,200; **British:** 35

Key actions The arrival of Beatty's First Battle Cruiser Squadron was decisive. Beatty's squadron sank the cruisers *Mainz*, *Köln* and *Ariadne*, and the destroyer *V187*, and damaged a further three other cruisers.

Key effects Beatty enhanced his reputation as a fighting seaman and the battle also influenced the British Admiralty's decision to appoint him as Commander of the Grand Fleet.

At the end of August 1914, General Joseph Joffre, the French commander-in-chief, ordered the French Fifth Army to launch a flank attack against the German First Army around Guise to take some of the pressure of the withdrawing British Expeditionary Force (BEF) to the west. The attack made little progress, but the Fifth Army's I Corps under General Louis Franchet d'Esperey temporarily stopped the advance of the German Second Army under General Karl von Bülow.

Joffre plans his counterattack

Bülow then called on the commander of the German First Army, Alexander von Kluck, to come to his aid. Kluck was under orders to advance to the west of Paris, but any support for Bülow would take his forces to the east of the capital. However, Kluck believed that the British were effectively defeated and that there were no sizeable enemy forces menacing his exposed right flank. Kluck could not reach Moltke, the chief of the German General Staff, for clarification, so moved to support Bülow on his own initiative. By 2 September his army was stretched out from the Marne River at Château-Thierry to the Oise River.

Thanks to air reconnaissance General Joseph Joffre, the French commander-in-chief, was aware of Kluck's change of direction and so planned for a massive counter offensive along the line of the Marne River by French and British troops.

BATTLE OF GUISE

Location France

Date 29–30 August, 1914

Commanders and forces German: Second Army (General Karl von Bülow); **France:** Fifth Army (General Charles Lanrezac)

Casualties German: 5,000; **French:** unknown

Key actions Despite French success in capturing Guise on 29 August, Lanrezac's position was precarious and liable to fall under the weight of heavy German assault. He was therefore ordered to withdraw, which he did on 30 August.

Key effects Guise served to delay the German advance towards Paris, time put to effective use by Joffre as he patched up the rest of the French line. Lanrezac was sacked by Joffre on 3 September, just before the Battle of the Marne.

On 5 September, the French and British launched their counterattack against the German forces along the Marne River between Paris and Verdun. In total, 1,071,000 Allied troops fought 1,485,000 German troops in a desperate battle to save the French capital. The offensive was successful, denying the Germans victory in 1914.

FIRST BATTLE OF THE MARNE

Location France

Date 6–12 September, 1914

Commanders and forces German: First Army (General Alexander von Kluck), Second Army (General Karl von Bülow), Fourth Army (Duke Albrecht), Fifth Army (Crown Prince Rupprecht); **French:** Third Army (General Maurice Sarrail), Fourth Army (General Langle de Cary), Fifth Army (General Louis Franchet d'Esperey), Sixth Army (General Michel Maunoury), Ninth Army (General Ferdinand Foch); **British:** British Expeditionary Force (Field Marshal Sir John French)

Casualties Germans: 250,000; **French:** 250,000; **British:** 12,733

Key actions Paris was saved on 7 September by the aid of 6,000 French reserve infantry troops ferried from Paris in streams of taxi cabs, 600 in all. This prevented the French Sixth Army from collapsing.

Key effects The original Schlieffen Plan had called for victory over France in the first few weeks of the war. The Battle of the Marne made this an impossibility. Germany now faced a war on two fronts.

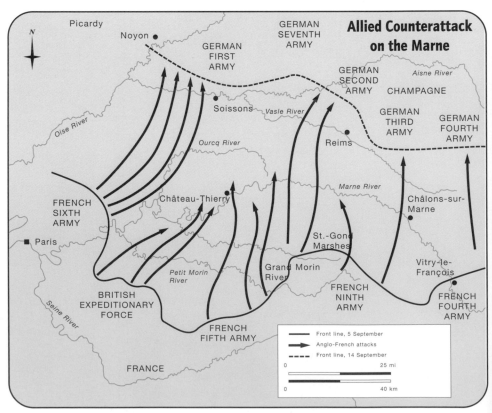

Allied Counterattack on the Marne

Front line, 5 September
Anglo-French attacks
Front line, 14 September

0   25 mi
0   40 km

FIRST BATTLE OF THE MASURIAN LAKES

Eager to capitalise on their recent victory against the Russian Army outside Tannenberg (see page 13), the Germans struck against General Rennenkampf's Russian First Army at the Masurian Lakes. The Germans again attempted to surround the Russians, but Rennenkampf launched a limited but successful counterattack, which allowed his battered forces to escape. Nevertheless, the action at the Masurian Lakes was another major German success.

Having roundly defeated the Russian forces menacing East Prussia, Generals Paul von Hindenburg and Erich Ludendorff afterwards rushed troops by rail to support the badly mauled Austro-Hungarians in Galicia. They believed, correctly, that the Russians were preparing to strike into Silesia, one of Germany's key mining and industrial centres. The rail transfer was speedy, allowing the creation of the new German Ninth Army under Hindenburg's personal command in the vicinity of Cracow.

German soldiers guard Russian prisoners awaiting the arrival of transportation to take them to their prison camps.

FIRST BATTLE OF THE MASURIAN LAKES

Location   East Prussia

Date   9-14 September, 1914

Commanders and forces   German: Eighth Army (General Paul von Hindenburg); **Russian:** First Army (General Rennenkampf)

Casualties   German: 40,000; **Russian:** 125,000

Key actions   Rennenkampf, fearing being outflanked, authorised a further orderly withdrawal on 9 September.

Key effects   East Prussia had been cleared of all Russian troops by 13 September and the battle largely removed any threat to German forces stationed in East Prussia itself.

BATTLE OF THE AISNE

Planning to exploit his success at the Battle of the Marne, Joffre ordered the French and British armies to attack the withdrawing German armies in what became known as the Battle of the Aisne. The main effort was by the British against the Chemin des Dames Ridge between Soissons and Craonne, in the direction of Laon. The attack met stubborn resistance. Joffre therefore called off the offensive.

Field Marshal Sir John French, the commander of the British Expeditionary Force.

BATTLE OF THE AISNE

Location   France

Date   13-28 September, 1914

Commanders and forces   German: First Army (Alexander von Kluck), Second Army (General Karl von Bülow), Seventh Army (General Josias von Heeringen); **French:** Fifth Army (General Louis Franchet d'Esperey), Sixth Army (General Michel-Joseph Maunoury); **British:** BEF (Field Marshal Sir John French)

Casualties   German and French: unknown; **British:** 12,000

Key actions   Allied attacks on 14 September were defeated by German machine-gun fire and heavy artillery in the defence of their positions.

Key effects   Fighting was abandoned on 28 September once it finally became clear that neither side, in particular the Allies, would be able to mount frontal attacks upon the well-entrenched positions of the enemy. Instead, both sides attempted to manoeuvre past the other in a northward movement, in the so-called Race to the Sea.

This clash was part of the Race to the Sea. The French Tenth Army (De Castelnau) began to assemble at Amiens from mid-September, and on 25 September began to push east. De Castelnau, under the command of Joffre, launched a frontal attack on the German lines near Albert after attempts to stretch the line northwards failed. The French were met with immediate resistance and counterattack as the German Sixth Army had reached Bapaume on 26 September and advanced to Thiepval on the 27th. The Germans were attempting to drive west to the English Channel, seizing the industrial and agricultural regions of northern France, cutting the supply lines of the British Expeditionary Force (BEF), and isolating Belgium.

However, neither side was able to achieve a breakthrough, and fighting around Albert ended around 29 September. The battle was a draw as both sides established trench lines in the area.

In September 1914 South African forces captured the wells of Sandfontein. The men had gone a long time in the hot sun without water, and the animals were near collapse from dehydration. As a result little protection was set up as all the men and animals stood gathering water. The entire formation was exposed to the surrounding heights, where German forces under General Heydebreck were located. Soon the South African position was being pounded by German artillery and raked by machine-gun fire. The South African artillery was soon knocked out. The Germans then moved their artillery forward, and after a few minutes the South Africans surrendered.

BATTLE OF SANDFONTEIN

Location   Namibia

Date   26 September, 1914

Commanders and forces   **German:** General Heydebreck (1,700 riflemen, mostly native, but all officers were German, 4 machine-gun teams and 10 artillery pieces); **British:** Colonel Grant (135 officers, 2,463 soldiers, 522 natives and 4 13-pounder guns)

Casualties   German 60, including 14 dead; British: 67, including 16 dead

Key actions   Only half an hour after the Germans brought their field guns forwards, the South Africans hoisted a white flag, and the engagement ended.

Key effects   Shortly after his great victory, Heydebreck died in an unfortunate accident. His replacement was Lieutenant Colonel Franke, whose skill in some respects surpassed that of Germany's other great generals of Africa.

FIRST BATTLE OF ALBERT

Location   France

Date   25-29 September, 1914

Commanders and forces   **German:** Sixth Army (Crown Prince Rupprecht); **French:** Tenth Army (General De Castelnau)

Casualties   unknown

Key actions   De Castelnau was met with immediate resistance and counterattack as the German Sixth Army had reached Bapaume on 26 September and advanced to Thiepval on the 27th.

Key effects   Neither side was able to make any decisive advances and the battle around Albert ended around 29 September as the fighting moved north towards Arras and Lille and into West Flanders. This confrontation and those to follow were deemed draws as the fighting settled into prolonged trench warfare.

French cavalry and infantry officers study the progress of the fighting in the Aisne River sector.

By the end of September the Germans had positioned heavy siege guns around Antwerp. On 1 October they opened fire, destroying Antwerp's outermost forts one by one. On 3 October the Germans had blasted a gap in the line of forts and were able to launch an assault that came close to forcing the abandonment of the city.

On 4 October the situation was temporarily restored by the arrival of the British Royal Naval Division. However, the next day the Germans breached the second and final line of modern forts around Antwerp and reached the inner line of redoubts, built in 1859 and totally unable to stand up to modern artillery. On 6 October, King Albert was forced to order the evacuation of his army. The bulk of the Belgian Army was able to escape along the coast to the southwest. Antwerp itself surrendered on 10 October. By then the garrison had been reduced to General Deguise, one sergeant and one private soldier, the rest of the army having escaped.

SIEGE OF ANTWERP

Location   Belgium

Date   28 September–10 October, 1914

Commanders and forces   German: German General von Boseler (5 divisions, 173 artillery pieces); Belgian: General Victor Deguise (145,000 troops in garrison)

Casualties   unknown

Key actions   The use of heavy guns such as the powerful Big Bertha (a 420mm siege howitzer) effectively put the Belgian forts out of commission. On 2 October the Germans succeeded in penetrating two of the city's forts. This weakened Belgian resistance and morale.

Key effects   German forces continued to occupy Antwerp until its liberation late in 1918. Most Belgian and Allied forces had, however, managed to escape the city west along the coast, subsequently taking part in the defence at Ypres in mid-October.

This battle was an attempt by the French to outflank the Germans in a northwesterly movement towards the English Channel. Designed to bypass the German forces by advancing along a line between Arras and Lens, the attack began on 1 October once the French had collected enough troops to make up General Maud'huy's new Tenth Army.

While initial progress toward Douai was good, effective counterattacks by Crown Prince Rupprecht's Sixth Army, transferred from Lorraine, obliged Maud'huy to order a withdrawal.

Nevertheless, in the face of heavy attacks by three corps of the German First, Second and Seventh Armies, the French managed to hold on to Arras, although Lens was lost to the Germans on 4 October. By this time fighting had subsided and the line began to stabilise once again.

FIRST BATTLE OF ARRAS

Location   France

Date   1–4 October, 1914

Commanders and forces   German: Sixth Army (Crown Prince Rupprecht); French: Tenth Army (General Maud'huy)

Casualties   unknown

Key actions   Effective counterattacks by the German Sixth Army, transferred from Lorraine, obliged Maud'huy to order a withdrawal.

Key effects   With the failure of French outflanking manoeuvres at Albert and Arras, activity moved farther north toward Flanders, where the Germans had some success.

The Belgian countryside was flooded to slow the German advance towards the English Channel.

BATTLE OF THE YSER

FIRST BATTLE OF YPRES

A German 150mm howitzer is readied to fire against Allied forces during the German advance into Belgium.

Field Marshal Sir John French ordered the British Expeditionary Force to advance toward Menin, Belgium, and Lille, France, on 18 October in the opening stage of the Battle of the Yser. However, the move was pre-empted by the Germans, who had begun a slow advance a few days earlier aiming to capture the Channel ports used by the British.

The British, with the aid of the French, were able to hold the German attack but at great cost. However, to the north, Belgian forces struggled to contain the enemy advance. Eventually, the Belgians opened canal and sea-defence sluice gates. This desperate act flooded a key area in the path of the German advance. On the 19th, the newly arrived British I Corps under General Sir Douglas Haig counterattacked around the Belgian city of Ypres. Haig's attack ended the German offensive.

BATTLE OF THE YSER

Location Belgium

Date 18–29 October, 1914

Commanders and forces German: Fourth Army (Duke Albrecht); French: 6,500 marines (Admiral Ronarch); Belgian Army (King Albert I)

Casualties German: unknown; French: 3,000; Belgian: 15,000, including 4,000 dead

Key actions On 22 October, a German division managed to form a bridgehead at Tervaete after a small band of troops managed to quietly cross a temporary footbridge over the Yser Canal without having fired a shot. This success forced the Belgians to retreat to the Diksmuide-Nieuwpoort railway.

Key effects The Belgians took the drastic step of opening the canal locks at Nieuwpoort on October 25. The result was a gradual flooding of the low country between the canal and the railway.

General Erich von Falkenhayn, the chief of the German General Staff, had steadily been building up the strength of the German Fourth and Sixth Armies around British-held Ypres to break through to the ports of Calais and Boulogne. Locally, the Germans enjoyed an advantage of six-to-one and were superior in medium and heavy artillery. The October offensive opened well and, despite French and British reserves being rushed to the sector, German units came close to breaking through southeast of Ypres on the 31st. Desperate fighting by the French and British eventually stemmed the tide.

In early November the Germans renewed their attempts to break through. Some progress was made and they took Dixmunde, to the north of Ypres, from the Belgians on the 11th. However, the British, who were bearing the brunt of the onslaught, finally halted the major German attacks on the same day.

The BEF suffers heavy casualties

Despite several German attacks over the following days, the worst of the fighting was over. The first snows fell on 12 November, heralding an end to the campaigning season. The First Battle of Ypres was a success for the French and British, but it had been won at high cost. Half of the British Expeditionary Force (BEF), for example, were casualties.

FIRST BATTLE OF YPRES

Location Belgium

Date 19 October–22 November, 1914

Commanders and forces German: Fourth Army (Duke of Wurttemberg), Sixth Army (Prince Rupprecht); French: IX and XVI Corps; British: BEF (Field Marshal Sir John French)

Casualties German: 130,000; British: 58,000; French: 50,000

Key actions On 11 November, two premier German divisions attempted to break through British lines just north of the Menin Road in the Nuns' Woods, only 6.4 kilometres (4 miles) from Ypres itself. The Prussian Guards and the 4th Division made for the town of Hooge; the attack lasting all day. Initially successful in creating a breakthrough, the Germans were slow in exploiting their gains. German indecisiveness enabled the British to assemble a motley collection of soldiers (cooks, officers' servants, medical orderlies, clerks and engineers) who stemmed the enemy advance and eventually drove them back to their own lines.

Key effects First Ypres was a foretaste of what was to come on the Western Front. Very high casualty figures from each participating army, combined with fighting and living in trenches, would soon come to dominate the stalemate on the Western Front.

BATTLE OF CORONEL

Admiral Maximilian von Spee, whose warships had been taking on coal from German colliers in Chilean waters, led his two heavy cruisers, the *Gneisenau* and *Scharnhorst*, and three light cruisers, the *Dresden*, *Leipzig* and *Nürnberg*, into battle in the late afternoon on 1 November in heavy seas.

Admiral Cradock's force, which had been hurriedly assembled to deal with Spee, consisted of two old heavy cruisers, the *Good Hope* and *Monmouth*, the light cruiser *Glasgow* and an armed former ocean liner, the *Otranto*. A fifth vessel, the ageing battleship *Canopus*, had been left behind in the Falklands, a British coaling station in the South Atlantic, because it could not keep up with the rest of Cradock's squadron.

Spee's two heavy cruisers used the longer range of their main guns to smash Cradock's cruisers and frustrate the manoeuvres of the British, who tried to get to close range to use their smaller guns. Both the *Good Hope* and *Monmouth* went down with all hands, including Cradock. The *Glasgow* and *Otranto* escaped under cover of darkness. The British quickly sent a squadron of warships to intercept Spee's warships.

BATTLE OF CORONEL

Location   Pacific Ocean, off Chile

Date   1 November, 1914

Commanders and forces   **German:** 2 armoured cruisers, 3 light cruisers (Vice Admiral Graf Maximilian von Spee); **British:** 2 armoured cruisers, 1 light cruiser, 1 armed liner (Rear Admiral Sir Christopher Cradock)

Casualties   **German:** 35, no ships lost; **British:** *Good Hope* and *Monmouth* were both sunk, with the loss of all 1,600 crew

Key actions   When he ran into the German force, Cradock could have escaped. Instead he chose to stay and fight, with disastrous consequences.

Key effects   Once news of the scale of the British defeat reached the British Admiralty in London, a decision was quickly taken to assemble a huge naval force under Admiral Sir Frederick Sturdee. This was promptly sent to destroy Spee's force, which it subsequently did, at the Battle of the Falkland Islands (see page 20).

BATTLE OF TANGA

A British amphibious assault directed against Tanga, a German-held port, was decisively defeated by Colonel Paul von Lettow-Vorbeck. Lettow-Vorbeck's force consisted of a few German companies and local troops. Tanga marked the beginning of a four-year-long guerrilla war by Lettow-Vorbeck, which would see him operate at will throughout East Africa, tying down increasingly large British and Commonwealth forces with little aid from Germany.

BATTLE OF TANGA

Location   Tanga, German East Africa

Date   3–5 November, 1914

Commanders and forces   **German:** 1,100 Askari (Colonel Paul von Lettow-Vorbeck); **British:** 8,000 Indian reservists (General Arthur Aitken)

Casualties   **German:** 81 wounded, 61 killed; **British:** 487 wounded, 360 killed

Key actions   Lettow-Vorbeck launched a counterattack on the evening of 4 November, backed by around 1,000 troops trained in the Prussian tradition. Rapidly overrunning the badly prepared British positions, Lettow-Vorbeck's forces forced the British to retreat.

Key effects   Lettow-Vorbeck gained much booty from the supplies left behind by the British in their hasty retreat, including machine guns, rifles and 600,000 rounds of ammunition.

German-officered local troops, known as askaris, *drill in German East Africa. Troops such as these defeated the British at Tanga.*

BATTLE OF KOLUBRA

BATTLE OF THE FALKLAND ISLANDS

Survivors from the German heavy cruiser Gneisenau *make for the British battleship* Inflexible *after the Battle of the Falkland Islands.*

Serbian forces under General Radomir Putnik, now supplied with ammunition by France, launched a major attack on the Austro-Hungarian forces inside Serbia. The Battle of Kolubra was a major Serbian victory. The Austro-Hungarian armies collapsed under the Serbian assaults and were thrown out of Serbia. The Austro-Hungarian commander, General Oskar Potiorek, was dismissed for this humiliating defeat and replaced by Archduke Eugene. Austro-Hungarian casualties in the campaign, which began in September, were enormous: roughly 50 percent, some 230,000 men. The Serbian casualty list in the campaign totalled 170,000 men out of 400,000 taking part.

BATTLE OF KOLUBRA

Location Serbia

Date 3–9 December, 1914

Commanders and forces Austro-Hungarian: Fifth and Sixth Armies (General Oskar Potiorek); Serbian: First Army (General Zivojin Misic), Second Army (General Radomir Putnik)

Casualties Austro-Hungarian: 273,000, including 43,000 prisoners; Serbian: 132,000

Key actions On 5 December, the First Serbian Army captured Mount Suvobor and broke through the positions of the Austrian Sixth Army.

Key effects The Austro-Hungarian war effort in Serbia had been dealt a fatal blow. The Serbs were essentially left alone throughout 1915, waiting for Allied reinforcements. They were themselves in no position to mount an offensive, having suffered huge losses in 1914.

Serbian troops launch an attack against Austro-Hungarian forces near Belgrade in November.

German Admiral Maximilian von Spee, fresh from his victory at Coronel, was surprised by a British squadron sent to intercept him.

On sighting the British, Spee ordered his warships to withdraw. However, two British dreadnought battleships, *Inflexible* and *Invincible*, gave chase supported by a number of armoured cruisers. As the two dreadnoughts emerged from Port Stanley harbour, the ageing battleship *Canopus*, which escaped the British defeat at Coronel, opened fire on Spee's ships from the harbour, where the vessel had been beached to create a steady gun platform.

Spee's position was hopeless: the British warships were faster and carried heavier armaments. The *Scharnhorst*, Spee's flagship, was the first ship to be sunk, followed by the *Gneisenau*. Two more German cruisers were then quickly sunk.

Spee's last warship, the light cruiser *Dresden*, escaped from the Falklands. However, it was cornered three months later in Chilean territorial waters by the *Glasgow* and *Kent*. Unable to evade its British pursuers, the last of Spee's squadron was scuttled by its crew.

BATTLE OF THE FALKLAND ISLANDS

Location South Atlantic Ocean

Date December 8, 1914

Commanders and forces German: 2 armoured cruisers, 3 light cruisers, 3 transports (Admiral Graf Maximilian von Spee); British: 2 battle cruisers, 3 armoured cruisers, 2 light cruisers and 1 grounded pre-dreadnought (Vice Admiral Sturdee)

Casualties German: 1,871 killed, 215 captured, 2 armoured cruisers and 2 light cruisers sunk, 2 transports captured and subsequently scuttled; British: 10 killed, 19 wounded, no ships lost

Key actions Early in the battle Sturdee managed to bring his powerful cruisers within extreme firing range.

Key effects German commerce raiding on the high seas was effectively brought to an end.

FIRST BATTLE OF CHAMPAGNE

German troops dig a trench in France late in 1914. By this time hopes of a quick German victory on the Western Front had disappeared.

Despite the worsening weather and the growing strength of the German defences, the French and British undertook a general offensive along the Western Front, from the North Sea to Verdun. They believed, correctly, that they outnumbered the Germans, who had rushed large numbers of men to the Eastern Front. However, they underestimated the strength of the German trench system or the excellent qualities of the German soldiers.

Most of the attacks ended by 24 December and little progress was made. Only in Champagne, where the French had made moderate gains at the expense of huge casualties, did the fighting go on over the winter months. The First Battle of Champagne continued into 1915, but elsewhere the fighting died down as both sides came to recognise that their belief in a swift victory was totally misplaced.

FIRST BATTLE OF CHAMPAGNE

Location France

Date 20 December, 1914–17 March, 1915

Commanders and forces German: Third Army (General Karl Einem); **French:** Fourth Army (General Fernand de Langle de Cary)

Casualties German: 90,000; **French:** 95,000

Key actions Though outnumbered in terms of troops, the German lines were efficiently entrenched and successfully demonstrated the superiority of modern defensive warfare, especially in their use of the machine gun.

Key effects Despite high losses for little gain, French Commander-in-Chief Joffre was convinced that the German lines were vulnerable to massed infantry assault, particularly given the knowledge that German forces were being transferred to the Eastern Front to conduct the battle against Russia. This would result in yet more costly frontal attacks against the Germans in 1915.

Germany's military planners and their enemies both faced a strategic dilemma in 1915: where was the war to be won? On the Western Front the Germans held French and Belgian territory and had no immediate need to attack. They could extend their defence lines, launch counterattacks and give up unimportant ground if necessary. Matters were different on the Eastern Front, where the fighting was more fluid and more suitable to the sweeping flanking attacks the Germans favoured.

If Russia was comprehensively defeated then the German forces on the Eastern Front could be sent west to deliver a knock-out blow against the British and French. Hindenburg and Ludendorff favoured an all-out onslaught to smash Russia, while Falkenhayn believed that the war could only be won on the Western Front and that victories against Russia would have only a limited overall impact. Hindenburg and Ludendorff, backed by Kaiser Wilhelm II, won the argument.

The British faced a similar dilemma. Some, mainly politicians, believed that the Western Front was a slogging match that offered little more than a growing casualty bill for negligible gain. They argued that action on other fronts, in the Middle East and the Balkans, might achieve more by knocking out of the war one or both of the two weaker Central Powers: Turkey and Austria-Hungary. Their opponents, chiefly senior military figures, argued that victory could only be achieved by defeating Germany on the Western Front. In 1915, the politicians had their way.

Italy joins the Allies

By now, Italy had joined the war. Some in Italy had sympathised with Austria-Hungary, seeing it as a great Catholic empire and a bulwark against the Eastern Orthodox Church. Some who favoured siding with Austria-Hungary and Germany hoped that this would allow Italy to gain colonial territory at the expense of France or Britain. Others wanted their country to join Britain and France, believing that the Habsburgs were traditional enemies of the Italians, and some believed

German troops advance following the Second Battle of the Masurian Lakes on the Eastern Front in February 1915.

that, because Britain 'ruled the waves', siding with Britain would prevent a loss of maritime trade. Some hoped for gain in territory at the expense of Austria-Hungary and perhaps the Ottoman Empire.

Britain and France were able to offer Italy a better bargain than were the Germans: Tyrol, Trieste and northern Dalmatia at the expense of Austria-Hungary, and a share of Asia Minor at the expense of the Ottoman Empire. Italy's political leadership came down on the side of joining Britain, France and Russia. Italy declared war on 23 May.

Stalemate at Gallipoli

British plans for 1915, and their answer to stalemate in France, was to strike at Gallipoli to open the straits to the Black Sea and their access to Russia. They also planned for offensives on the Western Front, believing that British public opinion would accept nothing less.

The British and French began bombarding gun positions on the Gallipoli Peninsula in February, and the first troops landed on 25 April. The Turks contained the invasions and in September stalemate set in. The Allied campaign ended in failure.

On the Western Front, defensive warfare continued to demonstrate its superiority over attack. French and British offensives gained little ground. At Neuve Chapelle in early March the British gained 2,000 metres (2,190 yards) and suffered 13,000 casualties. A French offensive at St Mihiel ended after 18 days of fighting with no meaningful gains and heavy losses in men. In April, against French colonial troops at Ypres, the Germans experimented with chlorine gas, which created gaps in the line. The British rushed troops to where the gas attacks had occurred, and they suffered thousands more casualties.

A French offensive at Artois raged from May to mid-June, the French suffering 100,000 more casualties and the Germans 75,000. On 25 September, after a summer of recuperation, the British and French tried another offensive. Little was gained and 142,000 men were lost, the Germans losing 141,000. On the Western Front in 1915 the British suffered a million casualties, the French about 1.9 million and the Germans about 612,000. These losses were all for no result.

BATTLE OF DOGGER BANK

BATTLE OF BOLIMOV

A clash between elements of the British Home Fleet and Germany's High Seas Fleet was partly brought about by public disquiet at the seeming ease with which German warships were bombarding ports on the east coast of England. On 23 January, Admiral Franz von Hipper's German battle cruiser squadron sailed to attack ports and the British fishing fleet. The British had already moved a force of warships under Admiral Sir David Beatty to Rosyth in southern Scotland, to intercept any German incursion into the North Sea. The interception of German radio traffic meant that the British knew about Hipper's raid.

Beatty and Hipper met at the Dogger Bank shoals roughly in the middle of the North Sea. Surprised by the British, Hipper ordered a withdrawal but was soon caught by Beatty's faster and better-armed warships. The *Blücher* was hit and sank shortly after midday. The rest of Hipper's fleet escaped.

The German Ninth Army under General August von Mackensen attacked towards Warsaw at the end of January 1915. The advance, known as the Battle of Bolimov, was opened by 600 artillery pieces bombarding the Russian positions with 18,000 poison gas shells – the first time poison gas had been used in the war. Russian counterattacks on 6 February recaptured ground lost to the Ninth Army at a cost of 40,000 casualties.

Bolimov was, in fact, a diversionary attack designed to mislead the Russians as to the true nature of the forthcoming German and Austro-Hungarian offensive. Directed by Field Marshal Paul von Hindenburg, the forthcoming offensive, scheduled to begin on 7 February, had been planned as a massive pincer attack.

BATTLE OF DOGGER BANK

Location   North Sea

Date   24 January, 1915

Commanders and forces   **German:** 3 battle cruisers, 1 armoured cruiser, 4 light cruisers, 18 destroyers (Admiral Franz von Hipper): **British:** 5 battle cruisers, 7 light cruisers, 35 destroyers (Admiral David Beatty)

Casualties   **German:** 1 armoured cruiser sunk, 1 battle cruiser heavily damaged, 954 killed, 80 wounded, 189 captured; **British:** 1 battle cruiser out of action, 1 destroyer out of action, 15 killed, 32 wounded

Key actions   Realising he was overpowered, Hipper attempted an escape, believing the British battle cruisers to be relatively slow. Beatty's cruisers, however, were notably faster than their German counterparts, and succeeded in reaching their extreme firing range by 09:00 hours.

Key effects   The battle boosted British morale and concerned Kaiser Wilhelm II enough to issue an order stating that all further risks to surface vessels were to be avoided.

BATTLE OF BOLIMOV

Location   Poland

Date   31 January, 1915

Commanders and forces   **German:** Ninth Army (General August von Mackensen); **Russian:** Second Army (General Smirnov)

Casualties   **German:** 20,000; **Russian:** 40,000

Key actions   The Russians launched a number of heavy frontal counterattacks by some 11 divisions, suffering 40,000 casualties and achieving little, German artillery repulsing the Russian attacks with ease.

Key effects   The Russians were aware that the Germans had attempted an innovation in their use of poison gas. Its failure was such that it was not greatly remarked upon at the time, and consequently was not widely reported to Russia's allies in the west.

German destroyers move cautiously while rescuing survivors from the Blücher, *a battle cruiser sunk at the Dogger Bank.*

DEFENCE OF THE SUEZ CANAL

SECOND BATTLE OF THE MASURIAN LAKES

British-officered Indian troops occupy shallow trenches during their defence of the Suez Canal against the Turks.

In World War I Egypt was officially part of the Ottoman Empire, but since 1882 it had been ruled by the British. Free and secure access to the Suez Canal was vital to the British Empire. The most valuable parts of the Empire were east of Suez, as were the dominions of Australia and New Zealand and their invaluable volunteers. At the start of 1915, crucial reinforcements were travelling through the canal on their way to the Western Front. At the start of 1915, the Turks decided to launch an expedition towards the Suez Canal. It would be commanded by Djemal Pasha, the Minister of Marine and one of the triumvirate that ruled the Ottoman Empire. He was also governor of Syria and Palestine and commander of the Ottoman Fourth Army. He was ably supported by his German chief of staff, Baron Kress von Kressenstein. In early February, the Turks attempted to cross the Suez Canal, but the attack was repulsed by British-officered Indian troops. The Turks fell back to Beersheba, Palestine, after suffering 2,000 casualties. The Suez Canal had been secured for the Allies.

DEFENCE OF THE SUEZ CANAL

Location Egypt

Date 2–3 February, 1915

Commanders and forces **British:** Indian Army (Major General A. Wilson–30,000); **Turkish:** Fourth Army (Djemal Pasha–25,000)

Casualties **British:** 200; **Turkish:** 2,000

Key actions On 2 February advance elements of the Ottoman Fourth Army reached the canal and began the assault. They were beaten back by an Indian force, subsequently reinforced by Australian infantry.

Key effects The Turks never again attempted to seize control of the Suez Canal.

Field Marshal Paul von Hindenburg began his pincer offensive against the Russians by sending his German Eighth and Tenth Armies against the Russian Tenth Army. The ambitious pincer attack involved an Austro-Hungarian attack in Galicia, towards Lemberg, and a German attack from East Prussia. It was hoped that the two pincers could meet east of Warsaw. The Eighth Army attacked first in the face of a blizzard. It nevertheless struck hard against the left flank of the Russian Tenth Army. On the 8th, General Hermann von Eichhorn's German Tenth Army attacked the Russian Tenth Army's right.

Disaster for the Russians

The Russians fought back hard but were forced back into the Augustow Forest, where only the heroic action of the Russian XX Corps prevented a complete disaster. The corps was forced to surrender on the 21st, but its action had allowed the Russian Tenth Army's other three corps to escape encirclement. Nevertheless, the Russian front line had been pushed back some 112 kilometres (70 miles). The Germans captured some 90,000 Russians during this action, which was known as the Second Battle of the Masurian Lakes. It was another major disaster for the Russians, but at least the Russian Army was still in being.

After their defeat at the Masurian Lakes, the Russians hastily formed the Twelfth Army under General Wenzel von Plehve, who launched a counterattack against the German right flank with some success on 22 February.

SECOND BATTLE OF THE MASURIAN LAKES

Location East Prussia

Date 7–22 February, 1915

Commanders and forces **German:** Eighth & Tenth Armies (Field Marshal Paul von Hindenburg), **Russian:** Tenth Army (General Thadeus von Sievers)

Casualties **German:** unknown; **Russian:** 56,000 plus 100,000 prisoners

Key actions On 9 February, the retreating Russians were attacked by the German Tenth Army – a newly created army sent to the east, consisting of eight divisions – from the north. This shattered the Russian right flank.

Key effects The battle had been a great tactical victory, but even Hindenburg admitted that it was a strategic failure. Three of the four Russian corps had escaped, although only after suffering massive casualties, and the Russian line had been restored.

On 10 March, Field Marshal Sir John French's British Expeditionary Force (BEF) launched a limited offensive at Neuve-Chapelle in Artois, northeastern France. Following a short bombardment by some 350 artillery pieces, four British and Indian divisions attacked along a 3,660-metre (4,000-yard) front. Early progress was comparatively good – Neuve-Chapelle fell, as did several lines of German trenches. However, ammunition shortages and rapid German counterattacks blunted the advance. The British dug in on the captured ground and beat off subsequent German attacks. British casualties totalled 11,500 men by the end of the offensive on the 13th. The British concluded that artillery fire was the key to success in trench warfare.

A Turkish advance on the British base at Basra was defeated at Shaiba. Although outnumbered two-to-one by 12,000 Turkish soldiers, the British troops inflicted some 3,200 casualties.

The Turkish attack on Basra approximately coincided with the British assault on Gallipoli. Turkish success in Mesopotamia would have encouraged anti-British sentiment in the Middle East, and would have been very damaging to British interests and morale elsewhere. The nature of the British victory in defeating this attack (virtually without artillery support or supply, and carried out by the sheer bravery of the infantry) was to become an unfortunate factor in boosting British confidence. It would lead them to disaster in Mesopotamia within a year.

BATTLE OF NEUVE-CHAPELLE

Location France

Date 10–13 March, 1915

Commanders and forces German: Sixth Army (Crown Prince Rupprecht); British: BEF (Field Marshal Sir John French)

Casualties German: 11,000; British: 11,200

Key actions Rupprecht launched a counterattack against the village of Neuve-Chapelle on 12 March, which halted the British advance.

Key effects After the failure of the Battle of Neuve-Chapelle, Sir John French complained that it failed due to a lack of shells. The 'Shell Scandal' clearly pointed the finger of blame at the government. This led to the 'Shell Crisis' of 1915, which brought down the Liberal British government under the premiership of Herbert Henry Asquith.

BATTLE OF SHAIBA

Location Mesopotamia

Date 11–14 April, 1915

Commanders and forces British: Indian Army forces (5,000); Turkish: 5,000

Casualties British: 1,200; Turkish: 3,200

Key actions On 14 April, the Shaiba garrison formed up and carried out a frontal assault against the Turks. They eventually smashed into the enemy positions, whereupon the Turks broke and fled in disorder.

Key effects The nature of the British victory in defeating the attack encouraged British commanders to believe, wrongly, that such tactics would always defeat the Turks.

Camouflaged British howitzers begin the 35-minute bombardment that heralded the opening of the Battle of Neuve-Chapelle.

SECOND BATTLE OF YPRES

The Second Battle of Ypres began with the first use of poison chlorine gas on the Western Front. Having no protection against the gas, several units holding the northern flank of the salient panicked and ran away, opening a gap in the front line 8 kilometres (5 miles) wide. A second gas attack took place the next day.

On 8 May, the Germans captured Frenzenberg Ridge and held it despite fierce counterattacks. On 24 May, a German attack at Ypres directed against the British-held Bellewaarde Ridge enjoyed early success, but many of the initial gains were lost to British counterattacks. The fighting ended on the 25th and marked the last act of the Second Battle of Ypres. The Ypres salient had been reduced to a depth of just 5 kilometres (3 miles).

The Anglo-French invasion of the Gallipoli Peninsula called for three initial landings: at Cape Helles, Ari Burna and a diversionary attack at Kumkale.

The landings on the peninsula did not go smoothly. At Cape Helles the British 29th Division came ashore at five beaches in the face of intense fire from the local Turkish defenders.

The Australian and New Zealand Army Corps (ANZAC) at Ari Burna came close to success. However, the prompt action of a Turkish officer, Mustafa Kemal, who rushed reserves to the sector just in time, prevented the ANZACs from taking their objective.

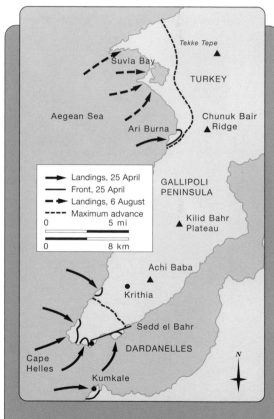

SECOND BATTLE OF YPRES

Location Belgium

Date 22 April–25 May, 1915

Commanders and forces German: Fourth Army (Duke Albrecht of Württemberg); British: Second Army (General Horace Smith-Dorrien)

Casualties German: 35,000; British: 59,000; French: 10,000

Key actions On 22 April, 5,700 canisters containing tonnes of chlorine gas were released at sunrise by the Germans against French Algerian and territorial division troops. The stunned Allied troops fled in panic towards Ypres, leaving a large gap in the line. However, the Germans had no reserves to send into the gap and capture Ypres.

Key effects The Allies quickly developed their own form of gas warfare.

LANDINGS AT HELLES & ANZAC COVE

Location Gallipoli Peninsula, Turkey

Date 25 April, 1915

Commanders and forces British: 75,000 (Sir Ian Hamilton) plus 18,000 French colonial troops; Turkish: 84,000 (Liman von Sanders)

Casualties British: 8,500; Turkish: unknown

Key actions Turkish troops quickly surrounded the Allied force and in addition were in possession of the heights above the beachheads.

Key effects Stalemate set in, along with a particularly unpleasant form of trench warfare similar to that experienced on the Western Front.

The commander of the British Expeditionary Force (BEF), Field Marshal Sir John French, was under severe pressure to support the major French offensive in Artois. Led by the corps of General Henri-Philippe Pétain, the French had advanced some 6 kilometres (4 miles) in 90 minutes at Artois to reach the key Vimy Ridge, a vital piece of high ground, on 9 May. Mounting losses convinced Pétain, however, that further frontal attacks on the ridge would be too costly.

French ordered his First Army under General Sir Douglas Haig to attack Festubert. The British attacked under cover of darkness for the first time. The onslaught was preceded by a 60-hour bombardment of the German trench lines. There were early gains by the British, but a mixture of rain, mist and a stiffening of German resistance prevented any exploitation. In

A lone British soldier looks out across no-man's-land during the Battle of Festubert.

addition, the British shortage of artillery shells became increasingly acute.

The British attack at Festubert ended on 27 May. The British commander-in-chief, Field Marshal Sir John French, contacted the British government stating that there could be no further attacks until his stock of artillery shells was replenished. The British had won territory a mile in depth across a 2,700-metre (3,000-yard) front, but at a high price.

BATTLE OF FESTUBERT

Location France

Date 15–27 May, 1915

Commanders and forces **German:** Sixth Army (Crown Prince Rupprecht); **British:** First Army (General Sir Douglas Haig)

Casualties **German:** 5,000; **British:** 16,000

Key actions On 17 May, in the face of British gains, the Germans pulled back to their second line, 1,190 metres (1,300 yards) behind the original front line. The British could not break through this line.

Key effects The battle reinforced the view that the BEF had a serious deficiency of artillery, particularly heavy weapons, and shells, especially high explosive that was required to destroy trenches and strong points.

Austro-Hungarian troops man trenches high above the River Isonzo, from where they could fire down on Italian troops.

The Italians opened the First Battle of the Isonzo on 23 June, 1915, marking the beginning of a series of 12 engagements in northeast Italy along the border with Austria-Hungary that would continue until 1918. The offensive planned to capture the Austro-Hungarian port of Trieste, two-thirds of whose inhabitants were Italian. However, the Italians had to overcome considerable physical obstacles, chiefly the River Isonzo itself, which meanders along the border and is backed by very steep mountains.

The Italians, who initially outnumbered the Austro-Hungarians by around 2-to-1 in men and artillery pieces, made some progress in the opening phase of the battle. Their main offensive, which began on the 30th, ended in failure. Italian forces attacked on a 32-kilometre (20-mile) front, but gained only a single foothold on the east bank of the Isonzo.

A renewal of the attack on 5 July achieved little. The Italian armies, the Second under General Pietro Frugoni and the Duke of Aosta's Third, spearheaded the onslaught. Despite a superiority of 6-to-1, they advanced little more than 1.5 kilometres (0.9 miles).

FIRST BATTLE OF THE ISONZO

Location   River Isonzo, northeast Italy

Date   23 June–7 July, 1915

Commanders and forces   Austro-Hungarian: 115,000 (General Svetozar Boroevi); Italian: 225,000 (General Luigi Cadorna)

Casualties   Austro-Hungarian: 10,000; Italian: 15,000

Key actions   The Italian commander launched massed infantry assaults without first assembling sufficient artillery protection. These invariably failed, with heavy losses.

Key effects   Cadorna was determined to break the trench stalemate, which would lead to further battles on the Isonzo.

The Battle of Gully Ravine at Helles began on 28 June, 1915. British and Indian troops were despatched in an effort to reinforce a moderate advance made there a week earlier by French troops. They also hoped to capture Achi Baba. Ammunition and artillery were once again in short supply on the Allied side, but the troops initially made progress, successfully taking Turkish coastal trenches. A strong Turkish counterattack in the first week of July failed to remove the Allies from their coastal positions, but prevented them gaining any higher ground.

Australian infantry await the order to launch an attack against the Turks at Gallipoli.

BATTLE OF GULLY RAVINE

Location   Helles, Gallipoli, Turkey

Date   28 June–5 July, 1915

Commanders and forces   British: 29th Division (Major General Henry de Beauvoir de Lisle), plus Indian 29th and 156th Brigade of 52nd (Lowland) Division (total 20,000); Turkish: 13,000 (Faik Pasha)

Casualties   British: 3,800; Turkish: 14,000

Key actions   On 2 July, the 1st Turkish Division led by Lieutenant Colonel Cafer Tayyar Bey commenced another counterattack at 18:00 hours. Again, though they advanced to within 30 metres (100 ft) of the British trenches, the losses were unbearable. Men were melting away in front of machine guns. The attack continued through the night, to no avail.

Key effects   The battle of Gully Ravine marked the Allies' furthest advance at Helles. The British attempted no more major offensives there for the remainder of the campaign.

SECOND BATTLE OF THE ISONZO

The Italians and Austro-Hungarians clashed once again in the Second Battle of the Isonzo. After the first battle was called off, the lack of artillery fire by the Italians was noted and fixed. The commander-in-chief of the Italian Army, General Luigi Cadorna, had sent more artillery to the front in the hope of achieving the decisive breakthrough to Trieste. For their part, the outnumbered Austro-Hungarians had reinforced their positions with just two divisions – but it was enough.

The battle began with a shorter, more accurate barrage by the Italians, and their Second and Third Armies made some initial progress, taking 4,000 Austro-Hungarian prisoners by the 22nd. However, a lack of shells and heavy artillery combined to slow the advance, which broke down in front of the still intact Austro-Hungarian trench systems protected by barbed wire. The few gains that the Italians made were recaptured by the Austro-Hungarians.

Italian tactics

In 1915 Italian commanders attacked positions up and down the long Isonzo Front. By attacking everywhere, they were unable to concentrate anywhere. Their assaults were almost always uncoordinated, often piecemeal and usually mounted with inadequate artillery support. Also, since the Austrians occupied the higher positions, the attacks usually failed to surprise them since they observed the preparations.

SECOND BATTLE OF THE ISONZO

Location   River Isonzo, northeast Italy

Date   18 July–3 August, 1915

Commanders and forces   Austro-Hungarian: 130 battalions, 420 guns (Conrad von Hötzendorf); Italian: 260 battalions, 840 guns (General Luigi Cadorna)

Casualties   Austro-Hungarian: 45,00; Italian: 60,000

Key actions   The Italian Second and Third Armies made a number of small gains in the Carso following two days of often hand-to-hand fighting after 18 July, but were unable to maintain forward position gains around Gorizia.

Key effects   Cadorna consistently persisted with a policy of massed frontal infantry attacks against well-prepared defensive positions, despite clear evidence on the Western Front that such tactics were useless.

BATTLE OF NASIRIYEH

British cavalry on patrol in Mesopotamia. As well as the Turks, British and Empire forces had to battle the stifling heat.

Following the defeat of the Turkish forces, Sir John Nixon decided to take the town of Nasiriyeh to deny it to the Turks. He assigned the task to General George Gorringe of the 12th Indian Division, who initially selected the 30th Brigade together with supporting artillery and transport for the job.

The British faced a difficult task just approaching the town, sometimes using boats on the River Euphrates, sometimes having to drag their guns and equipment over land.

Bayonet attack

Following a heavy bombardment, the infantry moved forwards, led by the 1st Royal West Kents. The Royal Navy, under heavy fire, dragged an old barge into place to act as a bridge across an unfordable creek. In fact the barge stopped the flow of water and men were able to wade across the river towards Turkish positions. Once they were among the Turkish trenches, which were roofed with brushwood, the bayonet did the rest. The first line soon fell. The second line was attacked but the Turks stood firm. However, strong support from the gunboats proved too much for the Turkish infantry, who fled. The British entered Nasiriyeh soon afterwards.

BATTLE OF NASIRIYEH

Location   Mesopotamia

Date   24 July, 1915

Commanders and forces   British: 30th Brigade (General George Gorringe, 5,000); Turkish: 5,000

Casualties   British: 500; Turkish: 1,500, plus 1,000 taken prisoner

Key actions   With the assistance of the Royal Navy the infantry stormed and secured the Turkish positions. The combination of infantry and gunboat support was effective in overwhelming Turkish opposition.

Key effects   This victory made the British commander-in-chief, Sir John Nixon, determined to capture the city of Baghdad.

LANDINGS AT SUVLA BAY

In an attempt to break the deadlock at Gallipoli, the British launched an amphibious assault on Suvla Bay on the north of the peninsula, adjacent to the original landing beach at Ari Burna. The plan was to outflank the Turkish defenders to the south, who had confined the British to the tip of the peninsula. The landings were to be made in conjunction with an Australian and New Zealand attack against the high ground known as Chunuk Bair.

Although the ANZACs attacked with great determination, their few gains were won at a high cost. They briefly captured the summit of Chunuk Bair on 8 August, but a Turkish counterattack led by Mustafa Kemal evicted them two days later. The landings at Suvla were unopposed, but the local commander, Sir Frederick Stopford, failed to take advantage of the situation, allowing Turkish reinforcements to gain the high ground overlooking Suvla Bay.

LANDINGS AT SUVLA BAY

Location Suvla, Gallipoli Peninsula

Date 6-15 August, 1915

Commanders and forces **British:** 11th Division (Lieutenant General Sir Frederick Stopford—20,000); **Turkish:** 'Anafarta Detachment' (Major Wilhelm Willmer—1,500) plus reinforcements from the Fifth Army in the days following

Casualties **British:** 8,000; **Turkish:** 20,000

Key actions The landings were made during the night on 6/7 August. Having been made in pitch darkness, there was great confusion with units becoming mixed and officers unable to locate their position or their objectives. Later, when the moon rose, the British troops became targets for Turkish snipers. Attempts to capture Hill 10 failed because no one in the field knew where Hill 10 was. Shortly after dawn it was found and taken, the Turkish rearguard having withdrawn during the night.

Key effects A state of trench warfare set in from Suvla onwards. Stopford was sent home to London in disgrace in mid-August.

Australian troops advance at the run with fixed bayonets against Turkish troops at Gallipoli.

Turkish troops taken prisoner during a British attack on the Gallipoli Peninsula.

On 21 August, 1915, a major effort was made to capture the heights inland from Suvla Bay, beginning with Scimitar Hill (now Yusufcuktepe). It was the greatest battle of the Suvla Bay area, but it failed.

British, Australian, New Zealand and Gurkha troops were also engaged in heavy fighting around Hill 60, between Anzac Cove and Suvla Bay, until the end of August. At this time the Anzac Cove and Suvla Bay fronts were now linked. The fighting then died down while the future of the campaign was debated. The Turks had virtually exhausted their reserves. However, the lack of any decisive achievements on the peninsula convinced the Allies to consider withdrawal.

BATTLE OF SCIMITAR HILL

Location Suvla, Gallipoli, Turkey

Date 21 August, 1915

Commanders and forces **British:** 29th Division (General Henry de Beauvoir de Lisle—14,300); **Turkish:** General Mustafa Kemal

Casualties **British:** 5,000 (many of which were incurred after British artillery shrapnel resulted in surrounding bushes catching fire); **Turkish:** 2,600

Key actions The reserves sent by de Lisle (then temporary commander at Suvla) encountered heavy losses while charging uphill and were consequently thrown back.

Key effects The attack at Scimitar Hill was the last attempt by the British to advance at Suvla. British officers and the rank and file were now demoralised. The front line remained between Green Hill and Scimitar Hill for the remainder of the campaign until the evacuation on 20 December.

BATTLE OF LOOS

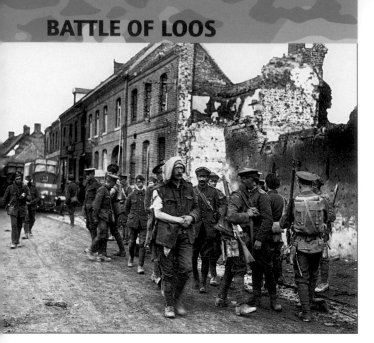

British wounded trudge through the streets of a shell-blasted town during the Battle of Loos.

As part of the Anglo-French offensives to begin simultaneously on the Western Front, General Sir Douglas Haig's First Army launched an attack between Lens and the La Bassée Canal, opening the Battle of Loos. The British, short of artillery ammunition, used gas for the first time in the war. However, adverse winds blew some of the gas back over the British lines and the terrain – strongly fortified villages and slag-heaps – made progress difficult.

The British 46th Division captured part of the German-held Hohenzollern Redoubt at the end of the battle and successfully beat off German counterattacks. The commander of the BEF, Field Marshal Sir John French, was blamed for the British failure.

BATTLE OF LOOS

Location France

Date 25 September–19 October, 1915

Commanders and forces German: (General Erich von Falkenhayn); British: First Army (I, IV, XI, and Indian Corps) (General Sir Douglas Haig)

Casualties German: 25,000; British: 50,000

Key actions On 26 September, the Germans poured in reserves to defeat the British, who had had to halt due to delays in the arrival of reserves. Advancing towards the Germans that afternoon without covering fire, they were decimated by repeated machine-gun fire; the Germans were astonished that the attack had been launched without adequate cover.

Key effects The British failure at Loos contributed to Haig's replacement of French as commander-in-chief at the close of 1915.

SECOND BATTLE OF CHAMPAGNE

Following a three-day bombardment by 2,500 artillery pieces, two French armies attacked the Germans on a 24-kilometre (15-mile) front, opening the Second Battle of Champagne. This was one of three major Anglo-French offensives to begin simultaneously on the Western Front. The aim was to give aid to Russia, which was under ferocious attack, and wear down German forces. Early gains were made – in the centre the French advanced some 2,700 metres (3,000 yards), and on the second day they broke through to the German second line. The fighting continued into November, but became increasingly bogged down.

French guards move German prisoners to the rear at the height of the Second Battle of Champagne.

SECOND BATTLE OF CHAMPAGNE

Location France

Date 25 September–6 November, 1915

Commanders and forces German: Third Army (General Karl von Einem); French: Second Army (General Pétain), Fourth Army (General de Langle de Cary)

Casualties German: 85,000; French: 143,567

Key actions The Germans had built a new second line of defences, 4.8 kilometres (3 miles) behind the first line. This alone would have made it almost impossible to achieve a breakthrough in a single day. Concrete machine-gun posts were built between the two lines. The rear lines were normally built on the reverse slopes of any available high ground, making it much harder for the Allied artillery to bombard the German second line.

Key effects The French Army suffered massive losses for little gain.

THIRD BATTLE OF THE ISONZO

The Italians again hammered away at the Austro-Hungarians defending the line of the River Isonzo as they continued their attacks towards Trieste. Despite having stockpiled over one million shells for the three-day barrage by 1,200 artillery pieces that opened their attack on the outnumbered Austro-Hungarians, the Italians made little progress. What little ground they gained was swiftly retaken. Heavy rain and mud also slowed the Italian offensive. The Italian attacks were called off on 4 November. Losses were large for almost no gains.

THIRD BATTLE OF THE ISONZO

Location   River Isonzo River, northeast Italy

Date   18 October–3 November, 1915

Commanders and forces   Austro-Hungarian: 137 battalions (plus 47 battalions of reinforcements), 634 artillery pieces (Svetozar Boroevic von Bojna); Italian: 338 battalions, 130 cavalry squadrons, 1,372 artillery pieces (Luigi Cadorna)

Casualties   Austro-Hungarian: 67,100; Italian: 40,400

Key actions   The Italians persisted in spreading the force of their attack too thinly throughout the Isonzo line. In addition, the Austro-Hungarians were in command of the high ground, could watch the Italians prepare their attack and made defensive plans accordingly.

Key effects   The battle was a costly failure. Cadorna would try again at the Fourth Battle of the Isonzo.

FOURTH BATTLE OF THE ISONZO

At the Fourth Battle of the Isonzo, the Italian offensive was heralded by an intense four-hour bombardment. Although attacking in force, the Italians made only limited gains and resorted to levelling one of their key objectives – the town of Gorizia – with artillery fire. The fighting died down on 2 December, with the Italians having made little further progress. Again, the list of casualties on both sides was high.

FOURTH BATTLE OF THE ISONZO

Location   River Isonzo, northeast Italy

Date   10 November–2 December, 1915

Commanders and forces   Austro-Hungarian: 155 battalions, 626 guns (Svetozar Boroevic von Bojna); Italian: 370 battalions, 1,374 guns (Luigi Cadorna)

Casualties   Austro-Hungarian: 32,000; Italian: 49,500

Key actions   At Mount Sei Busi, already the scene of four hard-fought attacks, a further five futile attacks were launched by the Italians.

Key effects   By the conclusion of the fourth Isonzo battle the Italians had penetrated a few kilometres into the Austro-Hungarian sector, but at great cost and without attaining any of the objectives defined earlier by Cadorna. Nevertheless, the Austro-Hungarian high command was sufficiently concerned by their losses that they requested military assistance from their German allies.

Specialised Italian mountain troops trek to their mountain-top positions in the Isonzo sector at the end of 1915.

In early 1916, the British had more than one million men in Belgium and France, while the French and German armies had resupplied their front-line troops. The stage was set for both sides to try to make the breakthrough on the battlefield that each hoped would assure them victory.

Instead, by the year's end both sides would lose nearly one million men with very little change in position of the front-line trenches. The battlefields became killing fields. In 1916, some of the most appalling battles in human history took place on the Western Front. The Battle of Verdun symbolised for the French the strength and fortitude of their armed forces and the solidarity of the entire nation. But it also bled the French Army white.

This tied in with the aims of German commanders, whose goal was not territory but to bleed the enemy to death. The battle lasted nine months and in the end the front lines were nearly the same, while more than 300,000 French and Germans were killed and more than 750,000 were wounded.

Slaughter – for no result

The British offered the same terrible sacrifice at the River Somme, where another million died, and at Ypres, in Belgium, a graveyard for half a million more. As the slaughter continued with no significant gains in territory by either side, the men in the trenches tried hard to keep their sanity. But cracks were appearing in the French Army.

By late 1916, Germany's military planners were becoming seriously short of manpower on the Western Front due to heavy losses, particularly at Verdun and on the Somme, and their commitments in several other war theatres. One of their solutions to the problem was to give up some territory on the Western Front and fall back to a more easily defensible – and shorter – front line. A shorter front would require fewer troops to defend it and free others for service elsewhere.

Central to this revised strategy was a new defensive doctrine known as defence-in-depth, which

French reinforcements are rushed to Verdun along the vital supply route known as the Sacred Way.

called for a comparatively thinly-held front line, backed by lines of more extensive defences stretching in depth to several kilometres. The aim was that the well-fortified but lightly-held front line would delay and break up any enemy attack, allowing time for fresh reserves to be rushed to the threatened sector. With fewer troops in the front line, it was believed that the massive preliminary bombardments by the enemy would cause fewer casualties than in the past.

The plan was the brainchild of Field Marshal Paul von Hindenburg and the defences were nicknamed after him. Preliminary work on the Hindenburg Line began in late 1916. The line, when completed in spring 1917, stretched from Arras, through St Quentin to Soissons, and shortened the Western Front by some 40 kilometres (25 miles). The contraction allowed around 14 divisions to be withdrawn from the front line.

The Eastern Front

On the Eastern Front, the Russians continued to launch offensives against the Austro-Hungarians and Germans, including the Brusilov Offensive of 4 June, 1916. This was timed to support the Battle of the Somme of July 1916 on the Western Front by drawing German troops to the east, and was initially a great success. The Russian General Alexei Brusilov advanced up to 160 kilometres (100 miles), and Romania joined the Allied powers. However, by the end of 1916 these early gains were lost and the Central Powers and their new ally Bulgaria had defeated Romania. Brusilov had achieved much, but the Russian Army had suffered almost a million casualties during the offensive. The Russian Army by this stage of the war was in a poor condition. Russian industry proved unable to continue manufacturing new equipment in sufficient quantities to replace such staggering losses, especially in small arms and ammunition. Indeed, some reports suggest that only 30 percent of Brusilov's troops had weapons, and his forces were demoralised. When German reinforcements arrived to bolster the Austro-Hungarian Army, Brusilov's success could not be sustained. As the bad news at home mounted, Russia slowly edged towards open revolution. And on the Western Front the French Army was near to mutiny.

The German offensive at Verdun was heralded by a nine-hour barrage from 1,240 artillery pieces, which fired both high-explosive and gas shells against a 13-kilometre (8-mile) section of the French front line to the north of Verdun. This was followed by an advance by 6,000 specialist German assault troops, some equipped with flamethrowers. These led the way for the main force of some 140,000 men from Crown Prince William's Fifth Army.

Pétain steadies the defence

The French lost some ground in the face of these heavy attacks. One of the key French positions at Verdun, Fort Douaumont, just 6 kilometres (4 miles) from the city, fell to German troops on 25 February. It was a major setback for the French, and the Germans appeared to be on the verge of victory. Late in the day, though, General Henri-Philippe Pétain took charge of the French forces at Verdun. Pétain re-invigorated the French troops and relied on defensive tactics rather than costly counterattacks, issuing the slogan 'Ils ne passeront pas' ('They Shall Not Pass'). He also ensured that the Bar-le-Duc road into Verdun – the only one to survive German shelling – remained open. It became known as *La Voie Sacrée* ('The Sacred Way'), because it continued to carry vital supplies and reinforcements into the Verdun front despite constant artillery attack. Pétain also introduced better coordination to French artillery fire, and instituted a system whereby units suffering heavy casualties were withdrawn from the fighting to rest and recuperate. French morale did not break.

Attack and counterattack

Nevertheless, the Germans kept attacking. On 9 April the Germans launched a major offensive against the high ground to the northwest of Verdun. Most of the attacks were repulsed by the French, but the Germans captured front-line trenches on *Le Mort Homme* Ridge ('Dead Man' Ridge).

On 24 October the French launched their counterattack. Its aim was to capture territory to the northeast of Verdun. Advancing under cover of mist, the French recaptured Fort Douaumont, taking 6,000 prisoners. German attacks were defeated. Within a few days, the French had forced the Germans away from key positions, including Forts Douaumont and Vaux. Although the fighting around Verdun would continue into 1917, this attack ended the main battle. Losses were enormous, but the German plan to destroy the French Army at little cost had failed.

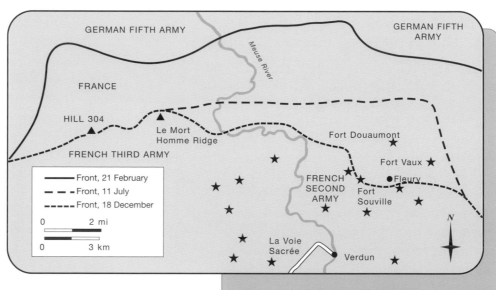

BATTLE OF VERDUN

Location Verdun-sur-Meuse, France

Date 21 February–18 December, 1916

Commanders and forces **German:** Fifth Army (Crown Prince William – one million troops); **French:** Second Army (General Langle de Cary, then Henri-Philippe Pétain – 200,000 at start of battle)

Casualties **German:** 434,000; **French:** 550,000

Key actions The appointment of Pétain was crucial to the French defence. He took action to ensure that an effective supply route to Verdun was maintained, designating a single artery road leading to a depot 80 kilometres (50 miles) to the west, Bar-le-Duc, and ensuring constant access by assigning columns of troops whose sole duty it was to maintain clearance of the road and to perform repairs as necessary. This saved the French position at Verdun.

Key effects Of the 330 infantry regiments of the French Army, 259 eventually fought at Verdun. The only real effect of the battle was the irrevocable wounding of both armies. No tactical or strategic advantage was gained by either side.

FIFTH BATTLE OF THE ISONZO

FIRST BATTLE OF LAKE NAROCH

In March 1915, the Italians launched the Fifth Battle of the Isonzo. The attack against the Austro-Hungarians was in part designed to help relieve some of the pressure on the French at Verdun. However, the Italian offensive was dogged by poor weather and their lack of artillery. Little ground was won or lost by either side in the battle, and the fighting in the sector died down at the end of the month.

In March the Russians launched a major offensive designed to aid the French, who were struggling to halt the major German offensive against Verdun. The Russian attack, which became known as the First Battle of Lake Naroch, involved a two-pronged advance into the Lake Naroch and Vilna areas. These were heralded by more than 1,200 artillery pieces bombarding German positions for eight hours. The Russian Second Army then moved against the German Tenth Army. Some 350,000 Russian soldiers faced just 75,000 German troops supported by 300 guns. Despite their numerical superiority, the Russians made little progress – gaining just 1,600 metres (1 mile) across a front of 3.2 kilometres (2 miles) for the loss of 15,000 men. So heavy were their losses, the Russians resorted to attacking under cover of darkness. However, subsequent Russian advances became bogged down in waterlogged terrain. The battle also failed to pull any German troops away from the Western Front.

FIFTH BATTLE OF THE ISONZO

Location   River Isonzo, northeast Italy

Date   9–15 March, 1916

Commanders and forces   Austro-Hungarian: 100 battalions (plus 30 in reserve), 470 guns (Svetozar Boroevic von Bojna); **Italian:** 286 battalions (plus 90 in reserve), 1,360 guns (Luigi Cadorna)

Casualties   Austro-Hungarian: 2,000; Italian: 1,900

Key actions   Halted almost as soon as it began on account of continuing poor weather, Cadorna had no opportunity to resuscitate what was really no more than a half-hearted attack before he was forced to deal with a large-scale Austro-Hungarian offensive in the Trentino.

Key effects   The fifth Isonzo battle may have been abandoned in haste but Cadorna was already planning the next, encouraged by promises of additional supplies of artillery from Italy's allies.

Russian prisoners are led away after the German victory at Lake Naroch in March.

FIRST BATTLE OF LAKE NAROCH

Location   Russia

Date   18–26 March, 1916

Commanders and forces   German: Tenth Army (General Eichhorn); **Russian:** Second Army (General Smirnov)

Casualties   German: 20,000; Russian: 100,000

Key actions   The Russian troops in the salients came under fire from three sides, which halted their advance and caused heavy casualties.

Key effects   During April local German counterattacks took back most of the lost ground.

The British relief force making for Kut-el-Amara made slow progress. Some 24 kilometres (16 miles) east of Kut, the Turks were forced to retreat just 450 metres (500 yards), but the British suffered heavy casualties and were little nearer to their objective. On 15 April, British aircraft began dropping food supplies to the besieged garrison. The garrison's commander, General Sir Charles Townshend, estimated that stocks of food would run out by the 29th. The British column heading for Kut, though, failed to break through Turkish lines.

BATTLE OF KUT

Location   Mesopotamia

Date   5–22 April, 1916

Commanders and forces   British: 30,000 (General George Gorringe); **Turkish:** 30,000 (Khalil Pasha)

Casualties   British: 4,800; **Turkish:** unknown

Key actions   On 6 April, the second day of the battle, attack after attack was made upon the Turkish trench lines. They were repulsed; 1,200 British casualties were incurred on 6 April alone, with additional losses suffered the next day and on 9 April. All attacks ended in failure.

Key effects   The British failure resulted in the surrender of the Kut garrison. General Townshend arranged a ceasefire on the 26th and, after failed negotiations, he simply surrendered on 29 April, 1916, after a siege of 147 days. Around 13,000 Allied soldiers survived to be made prisoners. The defeat weakened British influence in the Middle East.

British troops stand guard over Turkish prisoners captured during the attempt to rescue the British garrison at Kut.

On 15 May, the Austro-Hungarians launched a major offensive in the Trentino region on the north Italian border, which caught the Italians unprepared. The long-planned attack was opened on a 32-kilometre (20-mile) front and, despite the mountainous terrain, the Austro-Hungarians made some progress, chiefly thanks to their specialist mountain troops. The Austro-Hungarian Eleventh and Third Armies, commanded by Archduke Eugene, smashed through the lines of General Roberto Brusati's Italian First Army in the next few days.

The Austro-Hungarians maintained the momentum of their offensive in the Trentino by shifting the focus of their attacks towards the Asiago Plateau. Its capture would open the way into the lowlands of northern Italy. The Italians abandoned the plateau on the 29th.

However, the Austro-Hungarian offensive was slowing due to the problems of moving supporting artillery through the mountainous terrain. The offensive ground to a halt in June.

BATTLE OF ASIAGO

Location   Asiago Plateau, Trentino, today part of Italy

Date   15 May–10 June, 1916

Commanders and forces   Austro-Hungarian: Third and Eleventh Armies (General Archduke Eugene – 300 battalions, 2,000 guns); **Italian:** First and Fourth Armies (Luigi Cadorna – 172 battalions, 850 guns)

Casualties   Austro-Hungarian: 150,000; **Italian:** 147,000

Key actions   With the Austro-Hungarians advancing through his lines, Cadorna abandoned plans to continue the Fifth Battle of the Isonzo and redeployed half a million men to the Trentino by use of a highly efficient railway system. This had the effect of halting the Austro-Hungarians by 2 June.

Key effects   Due to the heavy casualties suffered at the battle, the Austro-Hungarians were never again able to launch a major offensive against the Italians without German assistance.

BATTLE OF JUTLAND

The British battle cruiser Queen Mary *blows up after being hit by German shells at the Battle of Jutland.*

The Battle of Jutland began in the early afternoon of 31 May. The main action opened shortly before 16:00 hours when Admiral Sir David Beatty's battle cruisers opened fire on German Admiral Franz von Hipper's battle cruisers.

Beatty attempted to sail south to cut Hipper off from his base in Germany. Hipper undertook a withdrawal to the southeast, hoping to lure Beatty into an unequal struggle against the main part of the High Seas Fleet. During this running fight Beatty was at a disadvantage as the low sun in the west highlighted his own ships, while the German battle cruisers were partly hidden by haze and mist. In the ensuing action Beatty came off worst: the *Indefatigable* was sunk. Twenty-five minutes later the *Queen Mary* was ripped apart by an internal explosion.

Beatty's own flagship, the *Lion*, also suffered severe damage, and his battle cruisers were perilously close to the battleships of the High Sea Fleet. He ordered his depleted force to turn away from the German fleet and headed north.

Meanwhile, Admiral Sir John Jellicoe had sent three battle cruisers to aid Beatty in his withdrawal. At 17:35 hours these opened fire on Hipper's ships, badly damaging the *Lützow* and hitting two light cruisers, the

Wiesbaden and *Pillau*. Jellicoe now carried out a manoeuvre that would place his battleships in a position that would give them an enormous advantage over the main German fleet – in effect cutting the Germans off from their bases and allowing the British fleet to pound their warships to destruction.

The High Seas Fleet faced a line of British warships some 14 kilometres (9 miles) long, but continued the fight. One of the first ships to succumb was Hood's flagship, the *Invincible*, which was blown apart by the *Derfflinger* and *Lützow*. The German fleet's commander, Admiral Reinhard Scheer, sensing the danger, opted to execute a turn away from the British, which would allow him to escape. However, Jellicoe attempted to block the German line of withdrawal.

The Germans retreat

To gain time for his main fleet, Scheer ordered his light units - torpedo-boats, destroyers and battle cruisers - to attack. Scheer's attempt to escape under the cover of darkness was successful, but his fleet had several losses. The old battleship *Pommern* was sunk by a torpedo; two light cruisers - the *Frauenlob* and *Rostock* - also sank; and the *Elbing* was sliced in half by the battleship *Posen* as it attempted to cross the bow of the larger ship. The battle cruiser *Lützow* had to be abandoned and was later sunk by a torpedo to prevent it from falling into British hands.

BATTLE OF JUTLAND

Location   North Sea, near Denmark

Date   31 May–1 June, 1916

Commanders and forces   German: High Seas Fleet (Vice Admiral Reinhard Scheer—99 ships); **British:** Grand Fleet: (Admiral Sir John Jellicoe—150 ships)

Casualties   German: 1 battle cruiser, 1 pre-Dreadnought, 4 light cruisers and 5 destroyers sunk; **British:** 3 battle cruisers, 4 armored cruisers and 8 destroyers sunk

Key actions   In the third phase of the battle, the German ships found themselves under bombardment from Jellicoe's battle fleet, which they had thought to be too far north to intervene. The heavy British guns quickly forced Scheer to order a retreat. The German fleet then found itself crossing in front of the British fleet, and in 10 minutes of gunfire suffered 27 heavy hits while only inflicting two.

Key effects   While the Royal Navy suffered more losses, the battle effectively ended any threat from the High Seas Fleet, which now knew it could not contest control of the North Sea with the Royal Navy.

This clash heralded the start of the Brusilov Offensive. Russian forces led by General Aleksey Brusilov, the Commander-in-Chief of the Southwest Front, launched a major offensive against the Austro-Hungarian and German armies in former Russian Poland and Austria-Hungary itself. The starting date for the offensive had been planned for 15 June following recent Austro-Hungarian successes against the Italians, whose high command had requested a Russian effort to draw Austro-Hungarian troops away from the fighting in Italy. The attack had been scheduled to coincide with the British onslaught along the Western Front's River Somme sector.

A promising start

Brusilov planned to advance on a broad front of some 320 kilometres (200 miles). His Third and Eighth Armies were ordered to strike against the Austro-Hungarian Fourth Army to the south of the Pripet Marshes. Farther south the Russian Seventh Army was directed against the Austro-Hungarian Seventh Army.

The operation was heralded by a bombardment from 2,000 Russian artillery pieces and early progress was excellent, particularly in the north and south, where the Austro-Hungarians virtually collapsed. Only in the centre, where the Russians faced German units, was the advance stalled.

Russian troops advance through barbed wire under fire during the opening moves of the Brusilov Offensive.

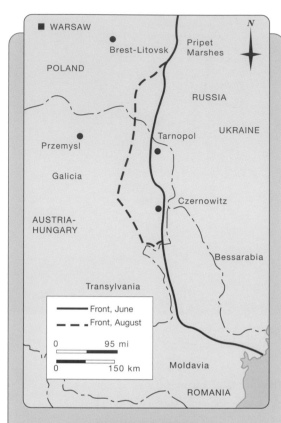

BATTLE OF LUTSK

Location Russia

Date 4–6 June, 1916

Commanders and forces Austro-Hungarian: Fourth Army (Archduke Josef Ferdinand–200,000); Russian: Eight Army (General Alexei Maximovitch Kaledin–150,000)

Casualties Austro-Hungarians: 150,000 (mostly taken prisoner); Russians: unknown

Key actions With 2,000 artillery pieces, the Russians created more than 50 breaches in Lutsk's barbed wire defences. The defenders fled in wholesale panic; however, extensive use of barbed wire around Austro-Hungarian fortified positions meant that many were unable to escape and were consequently taken prisoner by the Russians.

Key effects The loss of Lutsk effectively destroyed the Austro-Hungarian Fourth Army. The battle also heralded the launch of the successful Russian Brusilov Offensive.

BATTLE OF THE SOMME

The beginning of the Battle of the Somme. British infantry move forward slowly into a hail of enemy machine-gun fire.

The British offensive began at 07:30 hours on an intensely hot day following the firing of 224,000 shells in an hour. Shortly before the advance began, 10 huge underground mines were exploded beneath the German trenches, burying many of their occupants. Both the British commanders and the ordinary soldiers, most of whom were enthusiastic volunteers, believed that the first stage of the offensive, which became known as the Battle of Albert, would be an overwhelming success.

Disaster north of Albert

The advance took place along a front of some 40 kilometres (25 miles). There were early gains to the east and southeast of the town of Albert: Montauban and Mametz, where the British Fourth Army led by General Henry Rawlinson attacked, and west of Péronne, where French colonial troops made some progress. However, progress to the north of Albert was nothing short of disastrous. The attacking British infantry were confronted by uncut German barbed wire and intact defences, particularly around Beaumont Hamel and Thiepval. Advancing at a walk and burdened down with equipment, they met a wall of machine-gun fire. By the end of the day British casualties totalled more than 57,000, including 20,000 killed. It was the greatest loss ever suffered by the British Army in a single day's combat. German losses were around 8,000 men. The British also found it difficult to rush up reinforcements to the exhausted troops holding what little ground they had captured.

The British continued to attack German positions in the Somme sector until November. However, at the end of their attacks they had still not captured some of their first-day objectives. For example, they were still

5 kilometres (3 miles) from Bapaume. Despite having gained little territory, the British had inflicted equally massive casualties on the Germans during the fighting and contributed to their decision to withdraw to the Hindenburg Line.

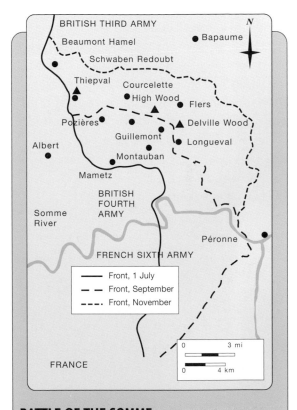

BATTLE OF THE SOMME

Location River Somme, Picardy, France

Date 1 July–18 November, 1916

Commanders and forces **German:** Second Army (General Fritz von Below); **British:** British Expeditionary Force (General Sir Douglas Haig); **French:** Sixth Army (General Marie Fayolle)

Casualties **German:** 680,000; **Britain and the Empire:** 419,654 casualties (125,000 killed); **French:** 204,000

Key actions On 1 July, the first day of the battle, as the 11 British divisions walked towards the German lines, the machine guns opened fire (despite the heavy bombardment, many of the German defenders had survived, protected in deep dugouts). Although a few units managed to reach German trenches, they could not exploit their gains and were driven back. By the end of the day, the British had suffered 57,000 casualties, of whom 20,000 were dead. Sixty percent of all officers involved on the first day were killed.

Key effects The British and French did succeed in capturing ground but advanced little more than 8 kilometres (5 miles) at the deepest point of penetration, well short of their original objectives. For the German Army, the Battle of the Somme damaged it beyond repair. It was never able to adequately replace its casualties with the same calibre of soldier that doggedly held his ground during most of the battle. In early 1917 it would withdraw to the Hindenburg Line defence system as a result.

The four battles fought on the Isonzo between August and November 1916 resulted in Germany entering the conflict between Italy and Austria-Hungary. In the Sixth Battle (6–17 August) the Italians gained some ground, chiefly Gorizia, which fell on 8 August. The Seventh Battle of the Isonzo (14–18 September) opened at 09:00 hours with the Italian Third Army attacking on a 10-kilometre (6-mile) front. The Italians made some early gains, but bad weather and strong Austro-Hungarian resistance combined to thwart any major progress. At the Eighth Battle of the Isonzo (10–12 October), the Italian Second and Third Armies attacked the Austro-Hungarian Fifth Army. Again, the fighting was indecisive. The Italians gained just 3 kilometres (2 miles) at a cost of 24,000 casualties. The Ninth Battle of the Isonzo (1–4 November) began with attacks by the Italian Second and Third Armies against Austro-Hungarian positions east of the town of Gorizia. Bad weather and heavy casualties (28,000 men) forced the Italian commander-in-chief, General Luigi Cadorna, to halt the attacks.

SIXTH TO NINTH BATTLES OF THE ISONZO

Location   River Isonzo, northeast Italy

Date   6 August–4 November, 1916

Commanders and forces   Austro-Hungarian: 14 divisions (General Svetozar Boroevic von Bojna); **Italian:** 20 divisions (General Luigi Cadorna)

Casualties   Austro-Hungarians: 103,000; **Italian:** 126,000

Key actions   With the failure of the Ninth Battle of the Isonzo, a lengthy rest period descended on the Isonzo Front – both sides were exhausted.

Key effects   The capture of Gorizia during the sixth battle boosted Italian morale. In the wake of this success the Italian government finally declared war on Austria-Hungary's ally, Germany, on 28 August, 1916.

Italian mountain troops move forwards against the Austro-Hungarians during the fighting along the River Isonzo.

BATTLE OF GUILLEMONT

Under mounting French pressure, and needing to offer aid to Romania, which had recently joined the war, General Sir Douglas Haig agreed to yet another major renewal of the Somme Offensive, which had degenerated into a series of localised battles since its beginning. Supported by a French attack south of Albert, the main British effort was directed against the village of Guillemont, which was captured by the 20th Division. However, attacks on German positions at High Wood and against the Schwaben Redoubt failed totally.

A British stretcher party takes a wounded soldier to a field hospital during the Battle of Guillemont.

BATTLE OF GUILLEMONT

Location France

Date 3–6 September, 1916

Commanders and forces British: 20th (Light) Division; **German:** Second Army (General Fritz von Below)

Casualties German: unknown; **British:** 2,000

Key actions On 3 September, the main assault on Guillemont itself was made by the 20th (Light) Division, two battalions of which crept forwards before zero hour and took the Germans by surprise. At noon the main line, including a brigade of the 16th (Irish) Division, advanced and after much difficult fighting (especially near the quarry and station) Guillemont was secured.

Key effects Further advances beyond Guillemont were hampered by fierce German fire from Ginchy and a stronghold called the Quadrilateral. It was clear that the capture of Ginchy (taken on 9 September) was essential in order to exploit recent hard-won gains.

BATTLE OF FLERS–COURCELETTE

British troops and a Mark I tank during a lull in the fighting around Flers-Courcelette on the Somme.

The British again attempted to break the deadlock at the Somme by launching what became known as the Battle of Flers–Courcelette (two villages to the northeast of Albert). Fourteen divisions were involved in the battle and tanks appeared on the Western Front for the first time. The advance went well, gaining some 2,285 metres (2,500 yards) along a 10-kilometre (6-mile) front. Both villages were captured, but the slow-moving tanks, despite causing initial panic among the German defenders, were far from successful. Many were knocked out, became stuck in mud and ditches or suffered mechanical failure during the advance.

BATTLE OF FLERS-COURCELETTE

Location France

Date 15–22 September, 1916

Commanders and forces German: Second Army (General Fritz von Below); **British:** Fourth Army (General Rawlinson), Fifth Army (General Gough)

Casualties unknown

Key actions This clash was the first time that tanks were used on the battlefield. Their use on 15 September at first caused panic among the Germans. With their help the British made initial gains of some 2 kilometres (1.25 miles) within the first three days of the battle - a remarkable achievement compared to other Western Front battles. The villages of Martinpuich, Flers and Courcelette fell to the Allies, as did the much sought-after High Wood.

Key effects Although tanks had not won the battle, Haig, the commander-in-chief, was suitably impressed and requested that 1,000 more be constructed.

In early 1917, bloody stalemate on the Western Front continued. On the Eastern Front, the Russian officer corps was increasingly demoralised by the poor progress of the fighting. The repeated catastrophes suffered by Russian field armies at the hands of the Germans destroyed what patriotism had existed three years earlier. By March 1917, some army units began ignoring their orders. After the tsar abdicated his throne that same month, a provisional government was formed with Alexander Kerensky at its head. He made a short-lived attempt to uphold Allied obligations by putting General Brusilov in command of yet another offensive against the German Southern Army in Galicia. But despite Brusilov's best efforts, his 1917 offensive only cleared a few mutinous Austrian formations out of the way before the German Army once again turned the tables on the Russians. This was the last straw for the Imperial Russian Army, which virtually disintegrated as open civil war swept across Russia.

The Germans move troops west

The collapse of the Russians on the Eastern Front threatened to free up hundreds of thousands of German troops for service on the Western Front. Only the slowness of the negotiations between the Germans and Russians prevented the immediate release to the west of huge numbers of German soldiers.

On the Western Front in 1917, after yet another failed French offensive, mutiny broke out in one French regiment and spread swiftly through 54 divisions. Many of the French soldiers swore that they would continue to defend their homeland, but they would no longer take part in offensives. Fortunately for the Allies, the mass mutinies did not become known to the Germans.

The British opened yet another assault at Ypres with a series of great mine explosions which totally disrupted the German lines. For once, the British inflicted more casualties than they received and pushed forward. However, by the time Haig had convinced his superiors that a breakthrough really had occurred, the

The battlefield of Third Ypres pictured with an abandoned British tank. Movement on such terrain was almost impossible.

Germans had patched up the lines and so yet another round of bloody fighting resumed. By the time Haig received his extra troops, the time for exploiting the breakthrough was long past, but the Third Battle of Ypres was launched anyway, causing one of the greatest slaughters of the war.

More disastrous still for the Allied war effort were the results of an Austrian offensive launched with German assistance in Italy in the autumn. In what became known as the Battle of Caporetto, the Italians in one blow lost 305,000 men; 275,000 of them surrendered as the Italian Army fell back 160 kilometres (100 miles) in panic. British and French divisions had to be rushed to Italy to keep the Italians in the war. By the time the United States was forced to enter the war in April 1917, the disasters on all the fronts had brought the Allies close to collapse.

On 2 April, 1917, U.S. President Woodrow Wilson addressed Congress, asking for a declaration of war against Germany. Just over two months earlier, on 31 January, the German government had announced its resumption of 'unrestricted submarine warfare'. With the announcement, German U-boats would without warning attempt to sink all ships travelling to or from British or French ports. Under the new strategy, U-boats had sunk three U.S. merchant ships with a heavy loss of American life in March 1917. Two days after Wilson's speech, the Senate overwhelmingly declared that a state of war existed between Germany and the United States. Two days later, the House of Representatives followed suit. The United States had entered World War I.

Enter the Americans

Since the United States went to war over the limited issue of Germany's submarine warfare, the Wilson administration could have taken only a naval role against German U-boats. However, pressure from both the British and French leaders urged Wilson to reinforce the Western Front that stretched from Belgium to Switzerland. Despite the carnage, the army's military leaders and planners saw the Western Front as the only place that the United States could play a decisive role in defeating Germany.

General Sir Frederick Maude, the commander of the British forces pushing north towards Baghdad, launched a major attack on the Turks at Kut-el-Amara on 22 February. He conducted a feint drive against the Turkish right to cover his forces crossing the River Tigris, and then unleashed powerful attacks on both Turkish flanks. The Turkish commander, Kara Bekr Bey, ordered his forces to retreat towards Baghdad following his defeat at what was the Second Battle of Kut. Kut-el-Amara was abandoned to the British on the 25th.

On 11 March, British forces, having brushed aside the Turkish Sixth Army under Khalil Pasha and after three days of skirmishing along the River Diyala, entered Baghdad. Keen to prevent the Turks from regrouping, Maude sent troops to scout along various rivers. However, the onset of intense summer heat eventually brought a halt to operations until September.

After Baghdad fell to the British on 11 March, 1917, there were still 10,000 Ottoman troops north of the city, led by Khalil Pasha. In addition, another 15,000 Ottomans under Ali Ishan Bey were being driven out of Persia by the Russians, and were attempting to join Khalil's forces in northern Iraq. The British commander, General Maude, decided that, in order to avert these threats, he had to take control of the Samarrah railway, running 130 kilometres (80 miles) north of Baghdad.

Operations began on 13 March, undertaken by 45,000 British troops. On 19 March, they conquered Fallujah, a crucial step towards the offensive's goal. The British continued their attacks until 23 April, when the town of Samarrah and its railway fell into their hands.

CAPTURE OF BAGHDAD

Location Mesopotamia

Date 11 March, 1917

Commanders and forces British: 50,000 (General Sir Frederick Stanley Maude); Turkish: Sixth Army (Khalil Pasha—25,000)

Casualties British: unknown; Turkish: 9,000 prisoners

Key actions On the morning of 11 March, British troops secured a crossing of the fast-flowing River Diyala, forcing the Turks to essentially abandon Baghdad.

Key effects As well as being a decisive propaganda blow for the Allies, the fall of Baghdad effectively ended Turkish activity in Persia.

British troops march into Baghdad following its capture from the Turkish Army.

THE SAMARRAH OFFENSIVE

Location Mesopotamia

Date 13 March–23 April, 1917

Commanders and forces British: 45,000 (General Sir Frederick Stanley Maude); Turkish: 10,000 (Khalil Pasha), plus a further 15,000 under Ali Ishan Bey retreating from Persia

Casualties British: 18,000; Turkish: unknown

Key actions On 31 March, Maude launched cavalry and infantry attacks against the town of Dogameh. They were successful, forcing the Turks to fall back to the Tigris/Adhaim Rivers junction.

Key effects The scale of his losses obliged Maude to pause and regroup pending a further advance in the autumn.

On 9 April, the British opened the Battle of Arras, intending to force the Germans to withdraw troops from the River Aisne sector of the Western Front, which was about to be attacked by the French commanded by General Robert Nivelle.

Three British armies were committed to the enterprise. In the centre, around Arras, lay General Sir Edmund Allenby's Third Army. To the north, poised to strike at Vimy Ridge, was the First Army under General Sir Henry Horne containing the Canadian Corps led by General Sir Julian Byng. South of Allenby, General Sir Hugh Gough's Fifth Army was to strike at the Hindenburg Line around Bullecourt. Facing the onslaught were the troops of the German Second and Sixth Armies.

Success, then stalemate

The British heralded their attack with a five-day bombardment. They achieved considerable gains on the first day, particularly the Third Army's Canadian Corps, whose spirited assault captured Vimy Ridge, and its XVII Corps, which advanced some 6 kilometres (4 miles). However, Gough made little progress.

The pilots of the British Royal Flying Corps suffered heavy losses due to the inferiority of their aircraft in comparison with the German Albatross D.III and the German tactic of diving on them from altitude. Some 33 percent of British pilots became casualties during April.

BATTLE OF ARRAS

Location France

Date 9 April–16 May, 1917

Commanders and forces German: Second Army (General von der Marwitz), Sixth Army (General von Falkenhausen); British: First Army (General Sir Henry Horne), Third Army (General Sir Edmund Allenby), Fifth Army (General Sir Hugh Gough)

Casualties German: 120,000; British: 160,000

Key actions Although the battle had become a stalemate by 11 April, the British commander-in-chief, Field Marshal Sir Douglas Haig, opted to continue the Arras offensive into the middle of May. His decision was made in part to draw the German Army's attention away from the sectors of the Western Front held by the French, whose armies were in disarray following widespread mutinies.

Key effects By the end of the offensive, the British had suffered more than 150,000 casualties and gained little ground since the first day. Despite significant early gains, they were unable to effect a breakthrough, and the situation reverted to stalemate.

On 17 April, British General Sir Archibald Murray again attempted to invade the Turkish province of Palestine by breaking through the enemy positions stretching between Gaza and Beersheba. He was told by the government to immediately invade Palestine and capture Jerusalem. As in the First Battle of Gaza fought in the previous March, the main effort was made by troops commanded by General Sir Charles Dobell. Dobell's frontal attack against well-entrenched Turkish forces ended in high losses and no gains. At no point were the Turkish lines seriously threatened. One British tank advanced the furthest, held part of the line for a short period, then retreated.

Murray is sacked

This action, the Second Battle of Gaza, had profound consequences on the British command structure in the region. First to pay the price of failure was Dobell, who was sacked by Murray. However, Murray's future was also in doubt as his recent failures at Gaza had angered the British government whose prime minister, David Lloyd George, had personally backed the attacks in Palestine and Sinai.

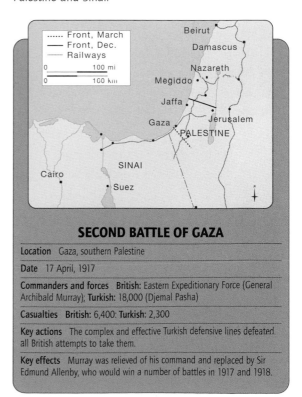

SECOND BATTLE OF GAZA

Location Gaza, southern Palestine

Date 17 April, 1917

Commanders and forces British: Eastern Expeditionary Force (General Archibald Murray); Turkish: 18,000 (Djemal Pasha)

Casualties British: 6,400; Turkish: 2,300

Key actions The complex and effective Turkish defensive lines defeated all British attempts to take them.

Key effects Murray was relieved of his command and replaced by Sir Edmund Allenby, who would win a number of battles in 1917 and 1918.

SECOND BATTLE OF THE AISNE

The opening of Nivelle's ill-fated offensive. French troops advance against the German-held Chemin des Dames Ridge.

On 16 April, General Robert Nivelle opened a major offensive that he had promised would smash the German defenders on the Western Front at little cost. The French advance took place along a front of some 65 kilometres (40 miles) between Soissons and Reims, with the bulk of the troops committed to capturing the Chemin des Dames, a series of thickly-wooded ridges running parallel to the front line. The Germans were fully aware of the onslaught, as there had been little secrecy and they had captured plans for the attack. Shortly before it began, German aircraft destroyed many French balloons used for artillery observation and strafed French troops and tanks.

French troops were met by heavy artillery fire and well-defended machine-gun positions. Their losses were heavy. A day after the opening of Nivelle's offensive, French troops began to mutiny. The offensive continued until 9 May, but ended in total failure.

SECOND BATTLE OF THE AISNE

Location River Aisne near Paris, France

Date 16 April–9 May, 1917

Commanders and forces **German:** First Army (General von Below), Seventh Army (General von Boehm), 480,000 troops in total; **French:** Fourth Army (General Anthoine), Fifth Army (General Mazel). Sixth Army (General Mangin), 1.2 million troops and 7,000 artillery pieces in total

Casualties **German:** 168,000; **French:** 187,000

Key actions As the plans for the attack were well known to the Germans, the defences were extremely deep and strong (100 machine guns on every 1,000 metres of front). As a result, on 16 April the French suffered 40,000 casualties. The mass use of French Char Schneider tanks brought little advantage, with 150 lost on the first day.

Key effects The French commander-in-chief, Robert Nivelle, was relieved of his command because of this bloody failure. The battle also sparked widespread mutinies in the French Army.

TENTH BATTLE OF THE ISONZO

On 12 May, the chief of the Italian General Staff, General Luigi Cadorna, finally initiated the delayed Tenth Battle of the Isonzo in northeast Italy. The offensive had originally been timed to coincide with two attacks on the Western Front by the French and British in mid-April, but muddled planning and lack of organisation had combined to delay the Italian effort.

The Italians failed to make any significant gains in the face of mountainous terrain and stubborn Austro-Hungarian resistance. Despite the lack of success on the Isonzo Front, Cadorna resolved to continue his efforts to break through to the Austro-Hungarian port of Trieste.

Italian artillerymen attempt to place a 75mm gun on the summit of a mountain in the Isonzo Front sector.

TENTH BATTLE OF THE ISONZO

Location River Isonzo, northeast Italy

Date 12 May–8 June, 1917

Commanders and forces **Austro-Hungarian:** Fifth Army (Field Marshal Svetozar Boroevic von Bojna); **Italian:** Third Army (Luigi Cadorna)

Casualties **Austro-Hungarian:** 75,700; **Italian:** 157,000

Key actions An Austro-Hungarian counterattack, launched on 3 June by General Wurm with three fresh divisions, pushed the Italians back off Mount. Hermada, a crucial piece of high ground on the approaches to Trieste. Essentially this reversed the gains the Italians had made in the battle up to that date.

Key effects Another huge amount of Italian casualties resulted in a drop in morale among Cadorna's troops. Nevertheless, he was determined to attack the Austro-Hungarians again before they were reinforced by the Germans.

Austro-Hungarian warships commanded by Captain Miklós Horthy, later the dictator of Hungary, attacked several Italian vessels sailing off the Albanian coast. Fourteen were sunk before British, French and Italian warships intervened, forcing Horthy to withdraw. Horthy said of the encounter: 'The enemy had lost twenty-three net-trailing drifters, two transports, two destroyers, and one aeroplane. In addition, the enemy flagship *Dartmouth* was attacked by a German U-boat as she was entering the harbour of Brindisi and holed by two torpedoes. The French destroyer *Boutefeu*, going to the assistance of the *Dartmouth*, ran onto a mine released by the U-boat and sank. We had not lost a single vessel and the Straits of Otranto were once more open to U-boats. We had shown that the drifter blockade could be broken. The enemy, as can be gathered from statements made at a later date, recognised the danger and, for a long time, drifters operated only during the hours of daylight, so that U-boats were able to pass through the Straits of Otranto at night unhindered.'

BATTLE OF OTRANTO STRAITS

Location Adriatic Sea

Date 15 May, 1917

Commanders and forces Austro-Hungarian: cruisers SMS *Novara*, SMS *Heligoland* and SMS *Saida*, supported by the destroyers *Csepel*, *Balaton* and three U-boats (Admiral Miklós Horthy); **Allied:** the British cruisers *Dartmouth* and *Bristol*, together with four Italian and French destroyers (Rear Admiral Alfredo Acton)

Casualties The Austrians reached their home port at the Bocche di Cattaro (Boka Kotorska) with some battle damage. The returning *Dartmouth* was torpedoed by the German submarine *UC 25* (Austrian number *U 89*).

Key actions The Allied force should have easily overwhelmed the Austrian ships. However, *Aquila* was disabled by Austro-Hungarian gunfire. Two of the Allied destroyers suffered breakdowns and had to be left behind with escorts. *Bristol* meanwhile proved too slow for the chase, with the consequence that only *Dartmouth* and two destroyers were left to shell the Austro-Hungarians from a distance, *Novara* being forced to a standstill.

Key effects As a result of this battle the Italians regarded the Otranto Barrage as essentially indefensible.

Inside the cramped control room of a German U-boat operating in the Adriatic Sea. The clean-shaven crew is an indication that this photograph was taken dockside and not at sea.

Field Marshal Sir Douglas Haig's British forces launched an attack against the high ground of Messines Ridge in southwest Belgium on 7 June. Haig was planning to stage a major offensive between the North Sea and the River Lys in the hope of breaking through the German lines around Ypres to the north, but before he could contemplate such an attack the dominating ridge at Messines had to be captured.

The troops committed to the painstakingly-planned British attack were drawn from the Second Army, and in a day's fighting they captured the ridge at a cost of 17,000 casualties. The German defenders suffered 25,000 casualties, of whom some 7,500 were taken prisoner. The capture of the ridge paved the way for Haig's grand offensive, the Battle of Passchendaele, which began in late July.

German-held trenches that were captured by the British during the attack on Messines Ridge, Belgium.

BATTLE OF MESSINES

Location   Flanders, Belgium

Date   7–14 June, 1917

Commanders and forces   German: Fourth Army (General Sixt von Armin); British: Second Army (General Herbert Plumer); French: First Army (General Anthoine)

Casualties   German: 25,000; British: 17,000

Key actions   On 7 June, the British detonated the mines that had been laid under German lines in the previous weeks (21 mines – 600 tonnes of explosive). The loss of surprise in the use of a preliminary bombardment was entirely offset by the effect of the mines, 19 of which detonated and blew the crest off Messines Ridge, killing 10,000 German troops.

Key effects   This battle, one of the the most successful local operations of the war, greatly boosted Allied morale.

At the end of July Field Marshal Sir Douglas Haig launched what became known as the Third Battle of Ypres, or Passchendaele. His aims were ambitious: to smash through General Sixt von Arnim's German Fourth Army, push several kilometres along the coast and then swing north to capture the ports of Ostend and Zeebrugge, from where German submarines and destroyers were operating. Once the ports had fallen, Haig intended to recommence his drive to evict the Germans from Belgium.

The initial attacks were moderately successful, but strong German counterattacks limited British gains to around 3 kilometres (2 miles). In August the British halted temporarily to allow the waterlogged ground to dry. The focus of the fighting was around the village of Langemarck, which was attacked by General Sir Hubert Gough's Fifth Army. Progress was slow due to the difficult conditions and the stubborn German defence.

In September the focus of the British offensive switched to the south of the Ypres salient. Three battles followed: Menin Road (20–25 September), Polygon Wood (26 September) and Broodseinde (4 October). The British were aided by the drying out of the ground and Haig opted to continue. In October and November the British again attempted to capture the village of Passchendaele. The rate of advance was painfully slow due to the dreadful ground conditions and the extensive use of mustard gas by the enemy. The village fell on 6 November, effectively ending the offensive.

BATTLE OF PASSCHENDAELE

Location   Passchendaele, Belgium

Date   31 July–10 November, 1917

Commanders and forces   German: Fourth Army (General Arnim), Fifth Army (General Gallwitz); British: Second Army (General Herbert Plumer), Fifth Army (General Sir Hubert Gough); French: First Army (General Anthoine)

Casualties   German: 260,000; British: 310,000

Key actions   British attacks in the first few days of the battle were severely hampered by the onset of heavy rains, the heaviest in 30 years, which churned the Flanders lowland soil into a thick muddy swamp. Tanks got stuck fast in the mud and the infantry found their mobility severely limited. The very force of the preliminary bombardment had itself destroyed drainage systems, making the problem much worse.

Key effects   The battle highlighted the futility of the 'big push' type of attack, which launched hundreds of thousands of troops against strong defences in the hope that sheer numbers would bring victory.

At the end of September 1917, British and Commonwealth forces under the command of General Sir Frederick Maude advanced north along the River Euphrates and confronted the Turks at the Battle of Ramadi. The Turks were defeated and pursued by the British deep into central Mesopotamia. Maude's intention, once he had secured central Mesopotamia, was to drive north along the River Tigris in the direction of Mosul, a vital oil-producing centre.

Turkish prisoners captured by the British at the Battle of Ramadi in Mesopotamia are led to the rear.

BATTLE OF RAMADI

Location Mesopotamia

Date 28-29 September, 1917

Commanders and forces **British:** 15th Indian Division, 6th Cavalry Brigade (General Sir Frederick Stanley Maude); **Turkish:** garrison of 4,000

Casualties **British:** 1,000; **Turkish:** 3,500 (mostly taken prisoner)

Key actions Although the Turks were expecting an attack, the appearance of British armoured cars caused panic among the garrison, allowing troops of the 15th Indian Division to enter the town.

Key effects Ramadi was a relatively easy victory, which encouraged Maude to turn his attention to capturing Tikrit.

BATTLE OF CAPORETTO

Austro-Hungarian artillery firing a mixture of high-explosive and poison gas shells opened the Twelfth Battle of the Isonzo, also known as the Battle of Caporetto. In the previous month the Austro-Hungarians had been reinforced by several German divisions and specialist mountain units. Six of the German divisions and nine Austro-Hungarian had been formed into the new Fourteenth Army. The main target of the Fourteenth Army was General Luigi Capello's Italian Second Army.

The Italians near collapse

The opening barrage caused panic among many Italian units, whose troops discovered that their gas masks offered no protection against enemy gas. Advancing through rain and mist, and bypassing points of Italian resistance, the offensive made rapid progress. By the 25th the attackers were exploiting a 24-kilometre (15-mile) breakthrough in the Italian line, forcing the Italian commander-in-chief, General Luigi Cadorna, to consider withdrawing to the Tagliamento River.

However, Cadorna was unaware of the true extent of the breakthrough or the strength of the enemy forces he was facing, primarily due to poor communications with his forward units. The order to withdraw to the next defensible barrier was finally issued on the 27th. The battered Italian armies were regrouping across the Tagliamento by the end of the month. It had been a great Austro-Hungarian/German victory.

BATTLE OF CAPORETTO

Location   Isonzo valley, northeast Italy

Date   24 October–19 November, 1917

Commanders and forces   German/Austro-Hungarian: Fifth Army (Field Marshal Boroevic), Fourteenth Army (General Otto von Below), 410,000 in total; **Italian:** Second Army (General Capello—350,000)

Casualties   German/Austro-Hungarian: 20,000; **Italian:** 300,000 (mostly prisoners)

Key actions   On the first day of the battle, the Germans and Austro-Hungarians broke through the Italian Second Army's lines almost immediately. They progressed a remarkable 24 kilometres (15 miles) by the end of the day, creating openings in the Italian line with the use of grenades and flamethrowers.

Key effects   Cadorna was dismissed and the Allies promised Italy military help. Six French Army divisions and five British divisions were therefore sent to Italy immediately.

THIRD BATTLE OF GAZA

The British and Commonwealth forces commanded by General Sir Edmund Allenby launched the Third Battle of Gaza at the end of October. Allenby had decided on a new plan to break through the Turkish-held Gaza–Beersheba line. Rather than launch frontal attacks against the heavily entrenched Turks around Gaza on the coast, he opted to use three of his divisions to launch a feint attack against the coastal town, while the bulk of his forces drove inland against Beersheba to secure its vital water supply and turn the Turkish left flank. The key element was the rapid capture of Beersheba's water – without it, Allenby's mounted forces would not progress far in the heat.

The Turkish opposition

Allenby was opposed by some 35,000 Turks, chiefly the Eighth Army and elements of the Seventh Army commanded by German General Erich von Falkenhayn. Falkenhayn also had a small number of German machine-gun, artillery and technical detachments under his orders. However, his position was somewhat undermined by his long supply lines.

The attack on Beersheba lasted throughout the day, but culminated in a daring and successful charge by a brigade of Australian light cavalry at dusk. Remarkably, the brigade charged straight through the Turkish defences and machine-gun fire, taking Beersheba and its vital wells. The weak Turkish Seventh Army at Beersheba was forced into headlong retreat, leaving the Turkish left flank exposed to further British advances.

THIRD BATTLE OF GAZA

Location   Gaza, southern Palestine

Date   31 October, 1917

Commanders and forces   British: Egyptian Expeditionary Force (General Edmund Allenby—88,000); **Turkish:** Seventh and Eighth Armies (General Erich von Falkenhayn—35,000)

Casualties   British: 18,000; **Turkish:** 25,000 (including 12,000 prisoners)

Key actions   The British did not launch a mass frontal attack but instead assaulted the town of Beersheba. Following an all-day battle an Australian light horse unit finally penetrated the Turkish defences and secured control over the town's wells before the Turks could execute a prepared plan to contaminate them.

Key effects   Having won the battle, Allenby turned his attention to the capture of the city of Jerusalem.

CAPTURE OF TIKRIT

The capture of Tikrit was one of the final major engagements on the Mesopotamian Front. It was fought in the wake of the decisive combined Anglo-Indian success at the Battle of Ramadi in September 1917. Maude despatched General Alexander Cobbe at the head of two divisions further up the River Tigris to tackle newly established Turkish defensive positions some 13 kilometres (8 miles) north of Samarrah.

Before Cobbe could strike, however, the local Turkish commander, Ismail Hakki Bey, withdrew to a position directly in front of the town of Tikrit. There, heavily protected Turkish trenches defended the town.

Cobbe nevertheless attacked on 5 November, having been reinforced by a division of cavalry in the interim. Frontal attacks succeeded after three hours of fighting in taking the Turkish front line, although heavy British cavalry losses were incurred during a charge on the Turkish second line. Cobbe captured the town but found it stripped of supplies.

The funeral of British General Sir Frederick Maude at Baghdad. He died of cholera, probably as a result of drinking contaminated milk.

CAPTURE OF TIKRIT

Location Mesopotamia

Date 5-6 November, 1917

Commanders and forces British: two divisions (General Alexander Cobbe); Turkish: Tikrit garrison (Ismail Hakki Bey)

Casualties unknown

Key actions On 5 November, frontal attacks succeeded after three hours' fighting in taking the Turkish front line, although heavy British cavalry losses were suffered during a charge on the Turkish second line.

Key effects The British commander-in-chief, Sir Frederick Stanley Maude, died of cholera on 18 November. With his death, the British war effort was scaled back. Tikrit was the last major battle in Mesopotamia.

BATTLE OF CAMBRAI

British tanks on their way to the front to take part in the Battle of Cambrai in November.

The British Third Army under General Sir Julian Byng opened the Battle of Cambrai on 20 November. Byng's plan aimed to cut through the German positions between the Canal de l'Escaut and the Canal du Nord. Cavalry were to move forwards rapidly against Cambrai, while infantry units and tanks took Bourlon Ridge before advancing northeast to Valenciennes.

The main attack was spearheaded by 476 tanks, marking the first use of such weapons en masse in the war. The tanks led six of Byng's 19 divisions in an major advance along 8 kilometres (5 miles) of the front.

The early attacks were spectacularly successful: the Hindenburg Line was pierced to depths of 9–12 kilometres (6–8 miles). However, many tanks broke down, became bogged down in ditches or were smashed by German artillery at close range. The fighting continued into December, with the Germans launching a series of successful counterattacks.

BATTLE OF CAMBRAI

Location Cambrai, France

Date 20 November-6 December, 1917

Commanders and forces German: Second Army (General Georg von der Marwitz); British: Third Army (General Julian Byng)

Casualties German: 50,000; British: 45,000

Key actions The attack on 20 November was not preceded by a preliminary bombardment, which helped to ensure complete surprise. As a result, 8,000 prisoners and 100 guns were captured on the first day of the battle alone.

Key effects If ultimately the mass use of tanks had failed to achieve the desired breakthrough, it had nevertheless demonstrated the potential for targeted use of the tank in offensive operations.

The Germans spent the winter of 1917–1918 retraining their army. The basic battlefield unit was no longer to be the company or battalion, but the squad. Each squad of stormtroopers was to be a mix of machine gunners, grenade throwers and flamethrower troops supported by a few riflemen. It was hoped that the new battlefield tactics would break the trench deadlock on the Western Front.

The last great German offensive was launched on 21 March, 1918: Operation Michael. It was opened with an unprecedented 6,000-gun barrage that delivered a lethal gas attack deep into Allied lines. At one point, the Germans advanced 22 kilometres (14 miles) in one day, more than at any other time during the fighting in the West. During the first six weeks of fighting, the Allies lost 350,000 casualties, but more troops were rushed across the English Channel and U.S. units began arriving in great numbers. More German offensives followed, their spearheads advancing to within 90 kilometres (55 miles) of Paris. The Allies were forced to issue a backs-to-the-wall order.

The failure of the German gamble

The German troops, however, were quickly tiring from the prolonged effort and giving in to periods of looting. The economic blockade of Germany had cut off many vital supplies and on the home front many people were starving. Many German troops were chronically undernourished. Whenever they encountered Allied food stocks, much time was lost as these desperate troops gorged themselves. The last German offensive, an attempted pincer operation around Reims, was finally stopped with concentrated artillery and aircraft attacks. The final Allied assault was not long in coming.

The first attacks were made in July by the French west of Rheims. This was followed by a British offensive at the Amiens Bulge and a general offensive towards the Hindenburg Line. The Americans under General John Pershing attacked the St Mihiel Salient south of Verdun and then attacked through the Argonne west of

German stormtroopers move forward at the opening of Operation Michael, which began on 21 March, 1918.

Verdun as part of a general advance. The Germans were now steadily pulling back, and even though the Allies continued to suffer tremendous losses, they were inspired by the continued German retreat. The fighting ended when the Armistice was signed on 11 November. Germany had been defeated.

A war like no other

When World War I ended, the scale of destruction and the loss of life were unparalleled in human history. Unlike previous wars, the fighting had been conducted, to a lesser or greater degree, almost constantly. From August 1914 until November 1918 rarely a day went by when there was no military activity.

The ferocity of the fighting, chiefly due to the nature of the predominantly trench-bound war and the destructive weapons employed by the warring nations, was also previously unknown. It should be noted that all of the following figures for casualties are rough estimates.

Out of the 65 million troops mobilised by all of the combatant nations, some 8 million were killed and a further 21 million wounded. With regard to the Central Powers, the figures were: Germany, 11 million mobilised and 1.8 million dead; Austria-Hungary, 7.8 million and 922,000; Turkey, 2.8 million and 325,000; and Bulgaria, 1.2 million and 76,000.

The figures for those opposing the Central Powers were: France, 8.4 million mobilised and 1.36 million dead; the British Empire, 8.9 million and 908,000; Russia, 12 million and 1.7 million; Italy, 5.6 million and 462,000; the United States, 4.3 million and 50,000; Belgium, 267,000 and 14,000; Serbia, 707,000 and 45,000; Montenegro, 50,000 and 3,000; Romania, 750,000 and 335,000; Greece, 230,000 and 5,000; Portugal, 100,000 and 7,000; and Japan, 800,000 and 300.

The loss of life in combat was mirrored in civilian casualties on an also unparalleled scale. Some 6.6 million died, chiefly in Russia and Turkey, which accounted for two-thirds of the total. In the case of Turkey many of its 2.1 million civilian casualties were ethnic Armenians killed by Turkish forces in their campaign of genocide against the Christian minority.

General Erich Ludendorff planned a knock-out blow on the Western Front. He recognised that, with the imminent arrival of thousands of U.S. troops in France, Germany was likely to lose the war. However, he planned to strike first. He transferred 70 divisions of troops from the Eastern Front, where the turmoil following the Russian Revolution had effectively ended Russian involvement in the war. In the short term, therefore, Germany had a clear numerical advantage over the British and French.

Ludendorff's plan was to exploit the differences between the British and French strategies for facing any major German offensive. He believed the French would give priority to the defence of Paris, while the British were more concerned with defending the ports along the northern French coast through which their supplies and troops flowed. Ludendorff aimed to attack at the juncture between the French and British forces in northeast France.

The first use of stormtroopers

Three armies were to advance along an 80-kilometre (50-mile) front from Arras to St Quentin and La Fère. This zone was defended by the British Third Army under General Sir Julian Byng and General Sir Hubert Gough's British Fifth Army.

Ludendorff had 63 divisions earmarked for the attack, many led by elite stormtrooper units, while the British could muster just 26. The offensive was codenamed Operation Michael, but was also known as the *Kaiserschlacht* ('Kaiser's Battle'). It began with a sudden five-hour bombardment on the British by 6,000 artillery pieces. They fired both gas and high-explosive shells. Under cover of thick fog the Germans attacked, with the specially trained stormtrooper units leading the way. The surprise and shock of the onslaught overwhelmed the thinly spread British.

Gough's Fifth Army collapsed in total confusion, exposing the right flank of Byng's Third Army. However, Byng's forces, which were holding a narrower front than those of Gough, withdrew across the River Somme in good order. The attackers there, drawn from the German Seventeenth and Second Armies, made significantly smaller gains.

However, on 5 April, General Erich Ludendorff, the deputy chief of the German General Staff and instigator of Operation Michael, called a halt to the offensive as it was clear that he would not achieve a decisive victory along the Somme. His forces had advanced some 64 kilometres (40 miles) and inflicted around 240,000 casualties on the British and French. German losses were equally severe, particularly among the stormtrooper units that spearheaded the onslaught. Ludendorff now switched his offensive to another sector of the Western Front.

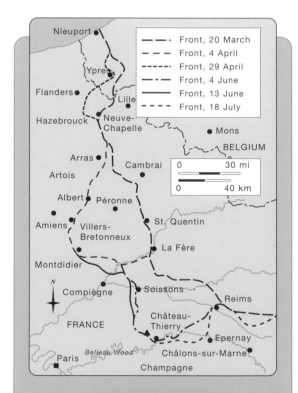

OPERATION MICHAEL

Location Somme region, France

Date 21 March–5 April, 1918

Commanders and forces **German:** Second Army (General Marwitz), Seventeenth Army (General Otto von Below), Eighteenth Army (General General Hutier); **British:** Third Army (General Byng), Fifth Army (General Gough)

Casualties **German:** 348,000; **British:** 236,000; **French:** 92,000

Key actions Although the Germans made some excellent advances, Byng's Third Army managed to limit the gains of the German Second and Seventeenth Armies in its sector.

Key effects On 3 April, Ferdinand Foch was made commander-in-chief of all Allied forces in France. This created a unified Allied command to combat the Germans. For the latter, the offensive had inflicted heavy losses on their specially trained stormtroopers.

LYS OFFENSIVE

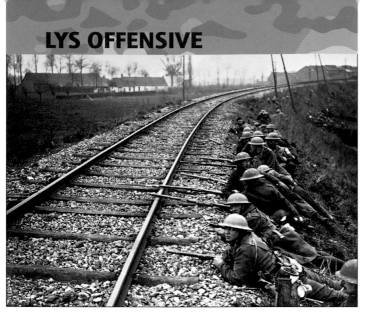

British troops take up position behind a railway embankment during the fighting along the River Lys.

General Erich Ludendorff opened the second of a series of attacks on the Western Front on 9 April. Operation Georgette was directed at the British Second and First Armies, which were separated by the River Lys. The offensive was to take place on a narrow front in the direction of the English Channel ports.

Following a three-day artillery bombardment, the attack began on 9 April. At first German forces were successful, creating a break in the British line 50 kilometres (30 miles) wide and closing in on one of their early objectives, the village of Hazebrouck.

By 17 April, though, British and French troops fighting around Ypres halted the German drive along the Lys. Although there was a series of attacks and counterattacks until the end of April, the German attempt to reach the ports of northern France had failed.

LYS OFFENSIVE

Location   Ypres, Belgium

Date   9–29 April, 1918

Commanders and forces   German: Fourth Army (General Sixt von Arnim), Sixth Army (General Ferdinand von Quast); British: First Army (General Horne), Second Army (General Plumer)

Casualties   German: 350,000; British: 305,000

Key actions   On 13 April, the Germans tried to capture the critical supply centre of Hazebrouck but were slowed by the defending British troops, before being stopped by the Australian 1st Division. This allowed the British and French to rush reinforcements to the area to halt the offensive.

Key effects   The Germans had failed to achieve a breakthrough, and instead occupied a vulnerable salient south of Ypres. Once again their casualties had been very heavy.

RAID ON ZEEBRUGGE

The British launched a surprise amphibious assault to curtail attacks by German submarines and destroyers operating in the English Channel from Ostend and Zeebrugge. The plan was to sink old warships across the canals that the enemy craft used to reach open water.

The attack on Zeebrugge began with British naval infantry trying to land from the cruiser *Vindictive* on the harbour's sea-walls and the destruction of an old submarine packed with explosives, the latter to isolate the German defenders of the sea-wall from the land.

As this action continued, three blockships – *Thetis*, *Intrepid* and *Iphigenia* – sailed into Zeebrugge's inner harbour. They were supposed to block the canal. *Thetis* grounded in the inner harbour; *Intrepid* and *Iphigenia* reached their target only to be sunk in the incorrect position. The attack on Ostend was even less successful, and another raid on Zeebrugge on 9 May also failed.

The aftermath of the British raid on Zeebrugge, Belgium, a base for German submarines and destroyers.

RAID ON ZEEBRUGGE

Location   Zeebrugge, Belgium

Date   23 April, 1918

Commanders and forces   German: unknown; British: 75 ships (Vice Admiral Sir Roger Keyes)

Casualties   German: unknown; British: 500

Key actions   The failure of the elderly British cruiser *Vindictive* to reach the entrance to the Bruges Canal to land troops who could then destroy the German shore batteries meant that their fire disabled three ancient British cruisers – *Thetis*, *Iphigenia* and *Intrepid* – packed with concrete which had moved into the inner harbour, preventing them from halting and scuttling themselves in their correct locations at the narrow entrance to the canal.

Key effects   The Zeebrugge raid did not hinder German operations from the port for more than a few days.

General Erich Ludendorff opened his third offensive on the Western Front in 1918 at the end of May. Ludendorff's aim was to stop the French from sending reinforcements to the aid of the British in northern France, where he was planning to attack again.

The German onslaught was heralded by a bombardment from 4,600 artillery pieces, which was followed by an attack by seven divisions on a front of 16 kilometres (10 miles). The Germans immediately captured the Chemin des Dames and advanced on the River Aisne, taking several intact bridges. By the end of the day the Germans had advanced 16 kilometres (10 miles). Although the offensive was intended to be limited, its early successes convinced the German high command to press towards Paris, just 130 kilometres (80 miles) distant. However, the French were being sent reinforcements by the commander of the American Expeditionary Force, General John Pershing.

American victory at Cantigny

U.S. forces undertook their first attack of the war on the second day of the German offensive along the River Aisne. The fighting centred on the village of Cantigny to the east of Montdidier. Elements of the U.S. 1st Division were pitched against the German Eighteenth Army. The U.S. troops captured Cantigny, taking 200 prisoners, on the 28th.

U.S. and French troops rush ammunition supplies to the front during the fighting along the Aisne River.

On 2–4 June, the U.S. 3rd Division under General J.T. Dickman went into action against the German troops threatening Château-Thierry on the River Marne. The division was able to prevent the German assault troops from crossing the Marne at Château-Thierry and then counterattacked with French support.

On 6 June, as part of the ongoing counterattacks against the German forces holding their recently won gains along the River Marne, the U.S. 2nd Division under General Omar Bundy attacked at Belleau Wood, a little to the west of Château-Thierry. Bundy's troops were facing the equivalent of four German divisions, yet after three weeks of fighting the wood was cleared.

THIRD BATTLE OF THE AISNE

Location   River Aisne near Paris, France

Date   27 May–6 June, 1918

Commanders and forces   German: First Army (General Bruno von Mudra), Seventh Army (General von Boehn); **British:** IX Corps (Lieutenant General Sir Alexander Hamilton Gordon); **French:** Sixth Army (General Duchene)

Casualties   German: 130,000; **French:** 98,000; **British:** 29,000

Key actions   By 3 June, the Germans were only 50 kilometres (30 miles) from Paris. However, problems with supplies and reserves, and troop fatigue, in addition to prolonged Allied counterattacks, halted the German advance at the Marne.

Key effects   General Duchene was dismissed by Pétain, but Pétain's own position came under threat, with his role being made subservient to that of the recently promoted and more able Allied Supreme Commander, Ferdinand Foch.

BATTLE OF THE RIVER PIAVE

The Austro-Hungarians, now fighting alone against Italy following the withdrawal of German forces to the Western Front, attacked in mid-June. Some 58 divisions were committed to a huge pincer attack across much of northern Italy. General Franz Conrad von Hötzendorf was ordered to take Verona, while General Borojevic von Bojna was to fan out across the River Piave, making for the River Adige and the city of Padua.

Austro-Hungarian fiasco

The attacks were far from successful. In the north the Tenth and Eleventh Armies were blocked on the second day of the advance and then counterattacked by the Italian Fourth and Sixth Armies. The Austro-Hungarians were forced to retreat, having suffered 40,000 casualties.

To the east the Austro-Hungarians attacked across the Piave on a wide front. Their Fifth and Sixth Armies gained 4 kilometres (3 miles) on a 24-kilometre (15-mile) front before running up against the defences of the Italian Third and Eighth Armies. The fighting in this sector continued over several days, with the Austro-Hungarians making some gains before a counterattack on the 18th forced them back.

The Austro-Hungarian offensive began to falter, partly due to the worsening weather and Italian air attacks, which undermined their flow of supplies. By the 22nd the Austro-Hungarians, who were in disarray, were forced back across the Piave.

BATTLE OF THE RIVER PIAVE

Location River Piave, Italy

Date 15–23 June, 1918

Commanders and forces Austro-Hungarian: Fifth, Sixth, Tenth and Eleventh Armies (Arthur Arz von Straussenburg); **Italian:** Third, Fourth, Sixth and Eighth Armies (General Armando Diaz), plus three British divisions and two French divisions

Casualties Austro-Hungarians: 60,000 dead, 90,000 wounded, 25,000 captured; **Italian:** 80,000

Key actions The Italians launched strong counterattacks as soon as the battle began, which cost the Austro-Hungarians 40,000 casualties within a week.

Key effects Before the battle the Austro-Hungarians had been suffering from equipment shortages and low morale. The failure of the offensive served merely to hasten the disintegration of the Austro-Hungarian Army on the Italian Front.

SECOND BATTLE OF THE MARNE

German troops cross a bridge destroyed by the French during the fighting along the River Marne.

The fifth German offensive of 1918 was another diversionary attack, this time in Champagne along the line of the River Marne, to draw the Allies' reserves away from northern France. The French, through a combination of aerial reconnaissance and talkative German deserters, were aware of the offensive and pre-empted it with a bombardment of their own. The German Third Army made little progress, being halted before noon on 15 July. Henceforth, the Germans concentrated their efforts to the west of Reims. By the 17th, however, Ludendorff accepted that his offensive has been stopped in its tracks.

The next day Allied forces counterattacked. In early August the Germans were forced to abandon Soissons and fall back to the line of the rivers Aisne and Vesle, abandoning the salient they had recently captured.

SECOND BATTLE OF THE MARNE

Location Marne region, France

Date 15 July–5 August, 1918

Commanders and forces German: First Army (General Mudra), Third Army (General Einem), Seventh Army (General Boehm), Ninth Army (General Eben); **French:** Fourth Army (General Gouraud), Sixth Army (General Degoutte); **British:** British Expeditionary Force (part of) (Field Marshal Sir Douglas Haig); **U.S.:** 85,000 troops

Casualties German: 168,000; **French:** 95,000; **British:** 13,000; **U.S.:** 12,000

Key actions The Germans broke through the French Sixth Army, but on 17 July French troops, supported by British and U.S. troops, halted their advance. This allowed the Allies to launch a devastating counterattack.

Key effects As a consequence of the disastrous result on the Marne, no further large-scale attempt to win the war was undertaken by the German Army on the Western Front.

Field Marshal Sir Douglas Haig's British Expeditionary Force (BEF) spearheaded the Amiens Offensive. The attack planned to clear parts of the railway running from Amiens to Paris, which had been held by the Germans since their Operation Michael.

The attack was preceded by a short bombardment and more than 400 tanks led the way forwards for the 11 British divisions earmarked for the first phase of the onslaught. The Anglo-French attack was overwhelmingly successful and the Battle of Amiens turned into a large-scale German defeat.

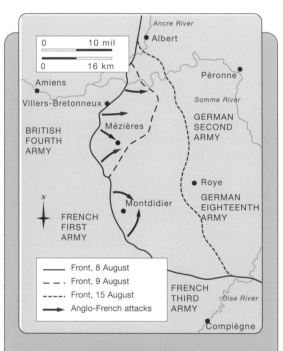

BATTLE OF AMIENS

Location Amiens, France

Date 8 August–3 September, 1918

Commanders and forces **German:** Second Army (General Marwitz), Eighteenth Army (General von Hutier); **British:** First Army (General Horne), Third Army (General Byng), Fourth Army (General Rawlinson); **French:** First Army (General Debeny); Third Army (General Georges Humbert)

Casualties **German:** 100,000, including 30,000 prisoners; **British:** 22,000; **French:** 20,000

Key actions In the first few hours of the battle six German divisions collapsed. Entire units began to surrender. Ludendorff called 8 August the 'Black Day of the German Army'. By the end of the day the Allies had advanced 14.5 kilometres (9 miles) over the entire 16-kilometre (10-mile) front. 16,000 prisoners were taken during the first day alone.

Key effects The unexpected extent of the British and Commonwealth armies' successes at Amiens encouraged Foch to plan the Meuse–Argonne Offensive for the end of September, with the intention of breaking the Hindenburg Line and forcing the Germans out of France.

British General Sir Edmund Allenby launched an attack against Turkish forces in Palestine, which were holding a line stretching inland from north of Jaffa on the Mediterranean coast to the valley of the River Jordan, in September 1918. The Turks were demoralised and short of supplies, chiefly because Arab forces under British liaison officer T.E. Lawrence had been disrupting the Hejaz railway along which their supplies flowed. Allenby had launched diversionary probes against the Turkish forces in the Jordan Valley, but actually intended to strike along the coast. To this end, real troop concentrations and supply dumps had been camouflaged in the sector, while nearer the Jordan dummy dumps and camps had been constructed.

Turkish forces collapse

The British offensive began at 04:30 hours with Allenby's artillery opening fire along a 104-kilometre (65-mile) front. British aircraft bombed railway lines and Turkish headquarters, effectively destroying their communications system.

The Turkish Seventh Army was virtually destroyed in the enveloping attack, while the Eighth Army attempted to escape eastwards. Both were harried by

British ground-attack aircraft. The retreat turned into a rout and some 25,000 Turkish prisoners were captured. The Turkish Fourth Army, positioned around the Jordan Valley, staged a withdrawal north in the direction of Damascus, but there was no hiding the scale of Allenby's victory.

BATTLE OF MEGIDDO

Location Palestine

Date 19-21 September, 1918

Commanders and forces **British:** Egyptian Expeditionary Force (General Sir Edmund Allenby—12,000 cavalry, 57,000 infantry, 540 field guns); **Turkish:** Fourth, Seventh, Eighth Armies (General Liman von Sanders—3,000 cavalry, 32,000 infantry, 402 field guns)

Casualties **British:** 5,000 killed and wounded; **Turkish:** 25,000 taken prisoner

Key actions The British attack along the Mediterranean coast on 19 September quickly broke through the overstretched Turkish line. This gap was exploited by Allenby's Desert Mounted Corps, which raced northwards in the direction of Megiddo and then swung eastwards for the River Jordan.

Key effects There was no longer any significant Turkish force available to oppose Allenby's advance north towards Damascus and beyond. On 30 October the Turks requested an armistice.

Indian lancers and their British officers pose for the camera during a break in their pursuit of the Turks in Palestine.

The First Army of General John Pershing's American Expeditionary Force launched the Meuse–Argonne Offensive to the north of Verdun. It was one of several attacks planned by France's Marshal Ferdinand Foch to drive the Germans from the defences of the Hindenburg Line and bring about their surrender.

The U.S. forces made rapid gains, advancing some 16 kilometres (10 miles) in the first five days of the offensive. French progress was somewhat less. The Germans rushed reinforcements to the sector.

On 28 September, the Group of Armies of Flanders under Belgium's King Albert also joined in the general offensive. The Germans abandoned the Hindenburg Line on 4 October. By 1 November, German resistance was collapsing. U.S. forces moved rapidly in the direction of Sedan. The offensive ended on the 11th with the signing of the Armistice.

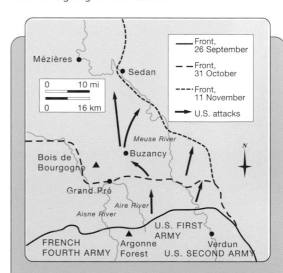

MEUSE-ARGONNE OFFENSIVE

Location Meuse Valley, France

Date 26 September-11 November, 1918

Commanders and forces **German:** Fifth Army (General Georg von der Marwitz); **French:** Fourth Army (General Henri Gourand); **U.S.:** First Army (General John Pershing)

Casualties **German:** 100,000; **French:** 70,000; **U.S.:** 117,000

Key actions The Americans launched a series of costly frontal assaults that broke through the main German defences between 14-17 October. By the end of October ,the Americans had advanced 16 kilometres (10 miles) and had finally cleared the Argonne Forest. On their left the French had advanced 32 kilometres (20 miles), reaching the River Aisne.

Key effects Coupled with British and French offensives in Belgium and around Lens, the assault through the Argonne was critical in breaking German resistance and bringing World War I to an end.

The Italian commander-in-chief, General Armando Diaz, launched an offensive against the Austro-Hungarian forces in northern Italy from his line along the River Piave. His aim was to penetrate the centre of the Austro-Hungarian line in the vicinity of Mount Grappa and capture the town of Vittorio Veneto.

The Italian forces consisted of 57 divisions, including three British and two French, backed by 7,700 artillery pieces. The Austro-Hungarians, whose morale was already badly shaken, deployed 52 divisions and 6,030 artillery pieces.

Italian breakthrough

The Austro-Hungarians were able to block the advance from Mount Grappa by the Italian Fourth Army, but the key part of the battle was around Vittorio Veneto. Initially, the battle went well for the Austro-Hungarian Sixth Army, which blocked the advance of the Italian Eighth Army as it tried to cross the River Piave. However, the Twelfth Army, commanded by French General Jean Graziani, gained a foothold on the Austro-Hungarian side of the Piave, as did the Earl of Cavan's British Tenth Army. By 28 October, both bridgeheads were secure.

British, French and Italian forces captured Vittorio Veneto, effectively dividing the Austro-Hungarian forces in northern Italy. After a week of fighting the offensive had penetrated to a depth of 25 kilometres (15 miles) along a front of 56 kilometres (35 miles). Austro-Hungarian forces then started to disintegrate. Italian troops reached the River Tagliamento on 2 November. The fighting officially ended on 3 November.

BATTLE OF VITTORIO VENETO

Location Vittorio Veneto, Italy

Date 23 October–3 November, 1918

Commanders and forces **Austro-Hungarian:** 52 divisions (Archduke Josef in the west and Boroevic von Bojna in the east); **Italian:** Third, Fourth, Eighth, Tenth and Twelfth Armies (General Armando Diaz); **British:** Tenth Army (Earl of Cavan)

Casualties **Austro-Hungarian:** 35,000 killed, 100,000 wounded, 300,000 captured; **Italian:** 5,800 killed, 26,000 wounded

Key actions On 30 October, the Italian Third and Tenth Armies succeeded in reaching the River Livenza and the Eighth Army took Vittorio Veneto, thereby splitting the Austro-Hungarian armies.

Key effects The battle resulted in the defeat of the Austro-Hungarian Army, signalling the wartime defeat of Austria-Hungary and the end of its empire. It was the final action fought on the Italian Front.

Italian troops take charge of an abandoned Austro-Hungarian position during the Battle of Vittorio Veneto.

FURTHER RESOURCES

PUBLICATIONS

Adams, Simon. *World War I (Eyewitness)*. Dorling Kindersley, 2004.

Arthur, Max, *Faces of World War I: The Great War in Words and Pictures*, Cassell, 2006.

Axelrod, Alan, *Complete Idiot's Guide to World War I,* Alpha, 2000.

Banks, Arthur, *A Military Atlas of the First World War*, Pen and Sword, 2002.

Borkan, Gary A., *World War I Posters*, Schiffer Publishing, 2002.

Clare, John D., *First World War (Living History)*, Gulliver Books, 1995.

De Groot, Gerard J., *The First World War (Twentieth-Century Wars)*, Palgrave Macmillan, 2001.

Gavin, Lettie, *American Women in World War I: They Also Served*, University Press of Colorado, 2006.

Gilbert, Martin, *The First World War: A Complete History*, Phoenix, 2008.

Granfield, Linda, *Where Poppies Grow: A World War I Companion*, Stoddart Publishing, 2002.

Hazen, Walter, *Everyday Life: World War I*, Good Year Books, 2006.

Horne, Sir Alistair, *The Price of Glory: Verdun 1916*, Penguin, 1994.

Junger, Ernst, *Storm of Steel*, Penguin Classics, 2004.

Keegan, John, *An Illustrated History of the First World War*, Hutchinson, 2001.

Keegan, John, *The First World War*, Vintage, 2000.

Kennedy, David M., *Over Here: The First World War and American Society*, Oxford University Press, 2004.

Kent, Zachary, *World War I: From the Lusitania to Versailles*, Enslow Publishers, 2011.

Lewis, Jon, *The Mammoth Book of Eyewitness World War I*, Avalon Publishing Group, 2003.

Meyer, G.J., *A World Undone: The Story of the Great War*, 1914 to 1918, Delacorte Press, 2007.

Neiberg, Michael, *The World War I Reader*, NYU Press, 2006.

Pope, Stephen, and Wheal, Elizabeth-Anne. *The Macmillan Dictionary of the First World War*, MacMillan, 1996.

Saunders, Nicholas, *World War I: A Primary Source History*, Gareth Stevens Publishing, 2005.

Steele, Philip. *In the First World War (Men, Women and Children)*. Wayland, 2010.

Stokesbury, James L., *A Short History of World War I*, Harper Paperbacks, 1981.

Strachan, Hew, *The First World War in Africa*, Oxford University Press, Oxford, UK, 2004.

Strachan, Hew, *The Oxford Illustrated History of the First World War*, Oxford University Press, 2001.

Tuchman, Barbara W., *The Guns of August*, Presidio Press, 2004.

Turner, Jason. *World War I (Wars Day by Day)*. Franklin Watts, 2008.

Weintraub, Stanley, *Silent Night: The Remarkable Christmas Truce of 1914*, Pocket Books, 2002.

Willmott, H.P., *World War I*, Dorling Kindersley, London, 2007.

Winter, J.M., *The Experience of World War I*, Papermac, 1989.

Zieger, Robert H., *America's Great War: World War I and the American Experience*, Rowman & Littlefield Publishers, Inc., 2001.

WEBSITES

www.firstworldwar.com
A multimedia history of World War I.

www.worldwar1.com
The people, places and events of World War I.

www.fordham.edu/halsall/mod/modsbook38.html
A large list of websites about World War I.

www.bbc.co.uk/history/worldwars/wwone
The causes, events and people of the conflict dubbed the 'war to end all wars'.

www.eyewitnesstohistory.com/w1frm.htm
Eyewitness accounts of some of the key events in the war.

www.ww1photos.com
A photographic history of World War I.

cybersleuth-kids.com/sleuth/History/Wars/World_War_I/index.htm
Cybersleuth Internet search guide for students.

www.kidskonnect.com/subject-index/16-history/287-world-war-i.html
Internet gateway site for young researchers.

www.iwm.org.uk/upload/package/95/index.html
Explore the Imperial War Museum's World War I collections.

INDEX

Page numbers in *italics* indicate illustrations.

1914 9–21
1915 23–33
1916 35–43
1917 45–53
1918 55–62

A

air warfare 14, 47, 48, 59, 60–1
Aisne, battles of the 15, 48, *48*, 58, *58*
Albert, battles of 16, 41
Allenby, General Sir Edmund 52, 60
alliances 7, *7*
Allies 23, 55
see also individual Allied countries
Amiens, Battle of 60, *60*
Antwerp, siege of 17
ANZAC (Australian and New Zealand Army Corps) 27, *29*, 31, *31*
Anzac Cove landings 27, *27*
arms race 6
Arras, battles of 17, 47
artillery *8*, *12*, 17, *18*, *26*, 28, 30, 32–3, 36, *48*
Asiago, Battle of 38
Australian and New Zealand Army Corps see ANZAC
Austria-Hungary 7, 9, 20, 23, 29–30, *29*, 33, 35, 37–8, 40, 42, 45, 48–9, 52, 59, 62

B

Baghdad, capture of 46, *46*
balance of power 6–7
Balkans 7
Basra 26
Beatty, Admiral Sir David 13, 24, 39
Beersheba 52
BEF see British Expeditionary Force
Belgium 9, 10, 11, *11*, *17*, 35
Bey, Kara Bekr 46
Bolimov, Battle of 24
Britain 7, 9, 23
air force 47
army 9, 12, 32, *38*, 41, *46*, 57
cavalry *12*, *30*
navy 9, 13, 17, 19–20, *20*, 24, 30, 39
British Empire 25, *60–1*
British Expeditionary Force

(BEF) 12, 14, 18, 26, 28, 60
Brusilov Offensive 35, 40, *40*
Bülow, General Karl von 11, 14
Bundy, General Omar 58
Byng, General Sir Julian 53, 56

C

Cadorna, General Luigi 30, 48, 52
Cambrai, Battle of 53
Cantigny, France 58
Caporetto, Battle of 45, 52
casualties 12, 18, 20, 23, 35, 55
Central Powers 23, 35, 55
see also individual countries
Champagne, battles of 21, 32
Chemin des Dames ridge 48, *48*, 58
Chile 19
chlorine gas 27
civilian casualties 55
constant attack doctrine 9
Coronel, Battle of 19
Cradock, Admiral 19

D

defence-in-depth doctrine 35
defensive warfare 23, 35
d'Esperey, General Louis Franchet 14
Diaz, General Armando 62
Dobell, General Sir Charles 47
Dogger Bank, Battle of 24, *24*

E

Eastern Front 23, 35, 45, 56
economic blockade of Germany 55
Egypt 25
Eugene, Archduke 38
Europe, 1914 7

F

Falkenhayn, General Erich von 18, 52
Falkland Islands, Battle of 20
Festubert, Battle of 28, *28*
Flers-Courcelette, Battle of 43, *43*
France 7, 9, 14, 17, 23, 35
army *12*, *16*, *32*, *34*, 35,

45
cavalry *16*
Francois, General Hermann von 11
French, Sir John 15, 18, 26, 28
Frontiers, Battle of the 10–12

G

Gallipoli 23, 27, *27*, 29, 31, *31*
gas attacks 23, 24, 27, 32, 36, 50, 52
Gaza, battles of 47, *47*, 52
German East Africa 19
Germany 7, 14–15, 17, 23, 35, 37, 45, 55–6
army *6*, *8*, *11*, *15*, *18*, *21*, 22, 41, *54*
navy 13, 20, *24*, 39
Gough, General Sir Hubert 56
Guillemont, Battle of 43, *43*
Guise, Battle of 14
Gully Ravine, Battle of 29
Gumbinnen, Battle of 11

H

Haig, Sir Douglas 18, 28, 32, 43, 50, 60
Heligoland Bight, Battle of 13
Helles landings 27, *27*
Hindenburg, General Paul von 11, 15, 23, 25, 35
Hindenburg Line 35
Hipper, Admiral Franz von 24, 39
Holland 9
Horthy, Captain Miklós 49
Hötzendorf, General Franz Conrad von 59
howitzers *8*, 17, *18*, *26*

I

Indian troops *25*, *60–1*
Isonzo, battles of the 29–30, *29*, 33, 37, 42, *42*, 48, *48*, 52
Italy 23, 30, 33, 37–8, 42, 45, 48, 52, 59, 62
army *33*, *42*, *48*
navy 49

J

Jellicoe, Admiral Sir John 39
Joffre, General Joseph 9, 10, 14, 15
Jutland, Battle of 39, *39*

45
cavalry *16*

K

Kluck, General Alexander von 12, 14
Kolubra, Battle of 20
Kut, Battle of 38

L

Lake Naroch, First Battle of 37, *37*
Lawrence, T. E. 60
Le Cateau, Battle of 12
Lettow-Vorbeck, General Paul von 19
Loos, Battle of 32, *32*
Ludendorff, General Erich von 11, 15, 23, 56–9, *57*
Lutsk, Battle of 40, *40*
Lys Offensive 57, *57*

M

Mackensen, General August von 24
Marne, battles of the 14, *14*, 59, *59*
Masurian Lakes, battles of the 15, *22*, 25
Maud'huy, General 17
Megiddo, Battle of 60–1
Mesopotamia 26, *30*, 38, 46, 51, 53
Messines, Battle of 50, *50*
Meuse-Argonne Offensive 61, *61*
mobilisation of armies 7
Moltke, Helmuth von 12
Mons, Battle of 12, *12*
Murray, General Sir Archibald 47

N

Namibia 16
Namur, siege of 11
naval battles 13, 19–20, 24, *24*, 39, *39*, 49
Neuve-Chapelle, Battle of 26

O

Operation Georgette 57
Operation Michael *54*, *55*, *56*, **56**
Otranto Straits, Battle of 49
Ottoman Empire 25

P

Pacific Ocean 19
Palestine 47, *47*, 52, *60–1*
Passchendaele, Battle of *44*, 45, **50**
Pershing, General John 61
Pétain, General Henri-Philippe 28, 36

Piave River, Battle of the 59
prisoners of war 15, 25, *31–2*, *37–8*, 51
Putnik, Marshal Radomir 20

R

Ramadi, Battle of 51
Rawlinson, General Henry 41
Romania 35, 43
Royal Navy 9, 13, 17, 19–20, *20*, 24, 30, 39
Russia 7, 9, 13, 15, 23–4, 35, 37
army *10–11*, 25, 35, 40, *40*, 45

S

the 'Sacred Way' *34*, 36
Samarrah Offensive 46
Sandfontein, Battle of 16
Schlieffen Plan 9
Scimitar Hill, Battle of 31
sea battles 13, 19–20, 24, *24*, 39, *39*, 49
Serbia 7, 20, *20*
Shaiba, Battle of 26
Somme, Battle of 41, *41*
South Africa 16
Stallupönen, Battle of 10

T

Tanga, Battle of 19
Tannenberg, Battle of 13, *13*
Tikrit, capture of 53
Trieste 29, 30
Turkey 7, 23, 25–7, 29–30, 31, 38, 46–7, 51–3, 60–1

U

U-boats 45, 49, *49*
United States 45, 58, 61

V

Verdun, Battle of 35, 36, *36*
Vittorio Veneto, Battle of 62, *62*

W

war plans 7, 9
Western Front 23, 35, 45, 56
Wilhelm II, Kaiser 7
Wilson, Woodrow 45

Y

Ypres, battles of 18, 27, *27*, *44*, 45
Yser, Battle of the 18

Z

Zeebrugge Raid 57, *57*